Cambridge |

M000078280

Elements in Austrian Economics
edited by
Peter Boettke
George Mason University

THE POLITICAL ECONOMY
OF PUBLIC PENSIONS

Eileen Norcross
George Mason University

Daniel J. Smith
Middle Tennessee State University

CAMBRIDGE
UNIVERSITY PRESS

CAMBRIDGE
UNIVERSITY PRESS

University Printing House, Cambridge CB2 8BS, United Kingdom

One Liberty Plaza, 20th Floor, New York, NY 10006, USA

477 Williamstown Road, Port Melbourne, VIC 3207, Australia

314–321, 3rd Floor, Plot 3, Splendor Forum, Jasola District Centre,
New Delhi – 110025, India

103 Penang Road, #05–06/07, Visioncrest Commercial, Singapore 238467

Cambridge University Press is part of the University of Cambridge.

It furthers the University's mission by disseminating knowledge in the pursuit of
education, learning, and research at the highest international levels of excellence.

www.cambridge.org
Information on this title: www.cambridge.org/9781009011624
DOI: 10.1017/9781009019965

First published 2021

A catalogue record for this publication is available from the British Library.

ISBN 978-1-009-01162-4 Paperback
ISSN 2399-651X (online)
ISSN 2514-3867 (print)

The Political Economy of Public Pensions

Elements in Austrian Economics

DOI: 10.1017/9781009019965
First published online: July 2021

Eileen Norcross
George Mason University

Daniel J. Smith
Middle Tennessee State University

Author emails for correspondence: Eileen Norcross (norcross@mercatus.gmu.edu); Daniel J. Smith (daniel.smith@mtsu.edu)

Abstract: Public pensions in the United States face an impending funding crisis in the wake of the financial crisis and the COVID-19 recession. Many cities and states will struggle to meet these growing obligations without major cuts in government services, reneging on pension promises, or raising taxes. This Element examines the development of the pension crisis through the lens of political economy. We analyze the knowledge and incentive problems inherent in the institutional structure, governance, and accounting of public pensions. We conclude by offering several institutional, governance, and reporting reforms to address the pension funding crisis.

Keywords: public pensions, fiscal illusion, Austrian economics, public choice

ISBNs: 9781009011624 (PB), 9781009019965 (OC)
ISSNs: 2399-651X (online), 2514-3867 (print)

Contents

1 Introduction

Public pensions in the United States face an impending funding crisis (Beerman 2013; Coggburn and Kearney 2010; Ricketts and Walker 2012). This is especially true in the wake of the Financial Crisis. Josh Rauh (2019) estimates that unfunded public pension debt in the United States exceeds $4.1 trillion, and the extent of the economic impact of COVID-19 on public pensions, at the time of this writing, remains to be seen. While no one foresaw the particular manifestations of the Financial Crisis or COVID-19 ahead of time, economists and financial experts do realistically expect periodic recessions. Public pensions, however, are not structured conservatively to withstand these expected ups and downs of the business cycle.

With annual pension payments already amounting to 8 percent of state and local tax revenue, these growing liabilities can crowd out other government expenditures, forcing state and local governments to cut essential government services (Kiewiet and McCubbins 2014; Novy-Marx 2014). According to a 2012 Chicago Booth IGM survey of economists, experts are concerned that, without reforms to their public pension plans, some states will have to drastically cut spending, default on pension benefits, or get a federal bailout (IGM Forum 2012). The possibility of a federal bailout represents a growing threat to federalism in the United States.

While many states guarantee or protect public employee pension benefits, high taxes can potentially drive residents away, leaving underfunded public pension systems with no option but to cut benefits *if* federal legislators reject bailouts due to the potential moral-hazard problems a federal bailout would create. Worse yet for these public employees, some of these underfunded public pension plans exempt their employees from social security benefits, meaning that these public employees are at even greater risk of retirement financial insecurity (Quinby et al. 2020).[1]

This Element examines the political economy of the United States public pension crisis.[2] More specifically, we detail the political economy problems inherent in defined-benefit public pension plans. We do so from an institutional perspective that factors in the knowledge and incentive problems faced by stakeholders. These political economy factors are what ultimately led to the development of this crisis. They also stand in the way of substantial reform.

---

[1] Public employees participating in social security are, of course, at risk to the extent to which social security is also underfunded (Kotlikoff and Burns 2012).

[2] While we focus on the United States, many of the political economy factors are likely generalizable to public pension plans elsewhere as well.

Current public pension institutions are built on the premise that stakeholders have the knowledge and motivations necessary to oversee and maintain these retirement promises made to public employees. In this Element we argue that defined-benefit public pensions thus systematically fail a robustness test because public pensions are unlikely to overcome the knowledge and incentive problems faced by stakeholders. To be successful, reforms will have to render public pensions robust to these knowledge and incentive problems.[3] Robust public pensions must be designed to be operable in a real world typified by deviations from the idealized assumptions.

To inform our understanding of the development of the pension funding crisis and reform efforts, we identify three primary institutional reasons for why public pensions as currently designed tend to fail the robustness test: (1) fiscal illusion, (2) governance, and (3) pension accounting and reporting.

Fiscal illusion is operative due to the presence of special interest groups and the ability of policymakers to misleadingly push costs into the future through the use of politically opportunistic accounting.[4] Thus, it is connected to both governance and accounting problems. Fiscal illusion enables the adoption of public pension structures and benefits beyond what taxpayers would be willing to support if they (the taxpayers) held a realistic assessment of the full costs of the program. Public employee unions are highly organized and thus very effective at lobbying for more generous pay and benefits for their members. With constitutional or legislative guarantees for funding their public pension, public employees lobby for increased benefits even when they might understand that the state or local government will struggle to procure the resources to meet those promises in the future. With their legal protection, they can rely on their lobbying power vis-à-vis the general public to help ensure that any future funding gaps will fall on future taxpayers at the local or federal level and not result in reduced benefits for themselves.

As mentioned, the governance structure of public pensions is replete with knowledge and incentive problems for stakeholders, decision makers, and technical experts. Elected officials, especially state and local politicians, often lack the expertise to accurately evaluate pension accounting or to gauge the full costs and benefits of potential reforms, especially when confronted with competing interpretations offered by actuarial auditors, employees' unions, and lobbyists. Policymakers also face incentive problems in that they have scarce time and budgetary dollars to allocate to understanding and properly funding

---

[3] For more on robust political economy outside the context of public pensions, see Boettke and Leeson (2004), Leeson and Subrick (2006), Levy (2002), and Pennington (2011).

[4] We adopt Stalebrink's (2014) apt phrase of "opportunistic accounting" throughout (also see Stalebrink and Donatella 2020).

public pensions. With the general taxpayer often being misled or unaware of pension finances, policymakers often have a strong incentive to cater to special interest groups.

Board members appointed to oversee public pension performance also face knowledge and incentive problems. Ex officio and appointed members are likely to make recommendations that advance their career opportunities in the eyes of taxpayers who elected them or the policymaker(s) that appointed them. Plan members serving the boards of public pensions, on the other hand, have the incentive to encourage the use of misleading actuarial reporting as it maximizes their opportunity for expanding additional benefits.

Pension plan CEOs, while well-informed, have the incentive to chase after high returns with riskier investments in order to keep contributions low and improve fund performance, especially during times of fiscal stress. While accounting and actuarial professionals are relatively highly informed, these groups face incentive problems as evidenced by the fact that they explicitly fought to avoid the implementation of accepted modern financial practices to public pensions. They went so far as to separate themselves from the Financial Accounting Standards Board by starting their own Governmental Accounting Standards Board (Flesher et al. 2019). Alongside state and local governments, accounting and actuarial professionals also lobbied to be excluded from the pension governance of the Employee Retirement Income Security Act of 1974 (Peng 2009, p. 88). They did so primarily to protect the current status quo of widespread opportunistic accounting.

Even public employees themselves may serve as a barrier to reform, despite the fact that it is their own retirement that is underfunded. This is because, as stated previously, most states constitutionally or legally protect their pension benefits. Politically, it is much easier to lobby for retirement benefits, with the costs pushed onto future taxpayers, than it is to lobby for current pay raises or other benefits, including retirement benefits that would properly be funded today, as that would require unpopular tax increases or budget cuts elsewhere (Anzia and Moe 2019; Bahl and Jump 1974; Bleakney 1973; Wagner and Elder 2021).

Throughout the remainder of this Element, we detail the precise political economy origins of the current pension crisis. We also provide recommended reforms grounded in robust political economy.

Section 2 uses the concept of fiscal illusion from public choice economics to explain how the funded health of public pensions became a crisis. Sections 3 and 4 respectively detail how governance and pension accounting and reporting contributed to the current state of this crisis and inhibit reform. Section 3 does this by addressing the governance problems inherent to defined-benefit public pensions and the knowledge and incentive problems faced by stakeholders. Section 4 examines the political economy of pension accounting and reporting. Section 5 examines the current state of pension reform and then provides specific accounting, governance, and structural reforms that incorporate concerns for robust political economy. Section 6 concludes by taking a broader look at the threat that the public pension crisis represents to federalism. We also discuss how the COVID-19 pandemic has further exacerbated the inherent problems with the current structure of public pensions in the United States.

2 Fiscal Illusion

While not a common household word, the concept of fiscal illusion is a primary factor behind the growth of unfunded pension liabilities (Hall and Hovey 1980; Inman 1982; Al-Bawwab and Smith 2020; Sneed and Sneed 1997). Fiscal illusion occurs when voters are led – through intentional deception or institutional design – to inaccurately assess the fiscal costs or benefits of an existing or proposed program (Da Empoli 2002; Oates 1988; Puviani 1903). Fiscal illusion can emerge whenever the costs or benefits of a program extend, especially in an obfuscated manner, into the future.

Policymakers seeking to create, support, or expand public programs to boost their odds of reelection can take advantage of fiscal illusion to provide explicit short-term benefits to electorally strategic groups through a misrepresentation of the long-term costs of the program to voters (Ostrom 1997, pp. 56–58 & 140). Voters can thus be led to tolerate or even endorse programs they would otherwise not if they had an explicit and accurate accounting of both the short- and long-term costs and benefits of the program.

Voter ignorance, which is undeniably a pervasive and inveterate feature of democracy (Brennan 2011; Caplan 2007; Somin 2016), is a necessary, but insufficient, condition for the emergence of fiscal illusion. This is because, on average, political ignorance will tend to cancel out due to the law of large numbers (Wittman 1995). Fiscal illusion, however, "implies a persistent and consistent behaviour" that does not average out (Oates 1988, p. 67). Thus, fiscal illusion requires "recurring, and presumably predictable, biases in budgetary decisions" on the part of voters (Oates 1988, p. 68). This means voters would have to be systematically biased (Caplan 2007) when it comes to a fiscal illusion.[5]

These biases could theoretically result in a public sector that is too small, where voters accurately perceive (or overestimate) the short-term costs of

---

[5] Caplan (2007) identifies four such biases among citizens in the United States; antimarket bias, antiforeign bias, make-work bias, and a pessimistic bias.

funding government programs but underestimate its long-term benefits (Downs 1960; Galbraith 1958). Fiscal illusion could also result in a public sector that is too large, if voters accurately perceive (or overestimate) the short-term benefits but underestimate its long-term costs. Figure 1 shows the possible outcomes from different combinations of biases on the part of voters regarding the costs and benefits of a government program.

Absent any systematic errors, the stable equilibrium should converge to optimal decision-making (Wittman 1995). Even in the presence of biases, entrepreneurial policymakers, or prospective policymakers, will have the electoral incentive to design programs and political messaging that will enable them to increase their electoral chances. Under- or overinvestment in a program based on biased beliefs on the part of voters opens a political opportunity for a policymaker to disabuse voters of their misperception and build a new winning coalition on the foundation of a more accurate understanding of the costs and benefits of the program, toward the optimal decision-making space. In a situation where there is overinvestment in the public sector, for instance, an entrepreneurial policymaker may have the electoral incentive to support programmatic or institutional reforms that would more accurately state the costs of programs (Holcombe 2002; Martin and Thomas 2013; also see Fink and Wagner 2013 and Wagner 2007).

While, as mentioned, theoretically fiscal illusion can result in too large or too small government programs, public choice economics suggests there is a strong tendency for policymakers to actively design and promote programs so as to maximize their perceived benefits and to minimize, or push into the future, their perceived costs (Buchanan 1960[2001], 92–97; Dell'Anno and Mourão 2012; Dollery and Worthington 1996; Mourão 2007; Oates 1988; Olson 1965; Ostrom 1997). There are two relevant insights from public choice that would explain why there is not a convergence toward optimal decision-making, especially when it comes to public pensions.

The first is the presence of special interest groups, especially well-connected and politically influential public employees. Due to the concentrated benefits they expect to receive from the program, special interest groups have a strong incentive to invest in lobbying policymakers (Olson 1965). Once a program is

	Overstated Benefits	Accurate Benefits	Understated Benefits
Overstated costs	Optimal political decision-making	Underinvestment in the public sector	Substantial underinvestment in the public sector
Accurate Costs	Oversized public sector	Optimal political decision-making	Underinvestment in the public sector
Understated Costs	Substantially oversized public sector	Oversized public sector	Optimal political decision-making

Figure 1 The sustainability of fiscal illusion

established, the tendency is for the beneficiaries to protect their privileged program, even after the benefits of the program have been capitalized, due to the transitional gains trap (Tullock 1975).[6] Established bureaucracies and public sector workers involved with the program are, similarly, vested in preserving the program and have the organizational structure to effectively lobby their position (Tullock 2005).[7]

Very few, if any, general voters, however, are concerned enough about underfunded public pensions as a single, predominant issue. Rather, they often have a wide range of additional political considerations that take priority over public pension issues (to the extent a general voter thinks at all about public pensions). With the costs of the program disbursed widely among all taxpayers, individual taxpayers have little incentive to invest in researching public pensions and lobbying for reforms.

This means there is little incentive for a policymaker to try to move toward optimal decision-making when there is an entrenched special interest group and general voter disinterest, as it would require immense political capital and resources to overcome special interest groups (public employees) with little, if any, electoral gain from voters. Thus, special interest groups severely limit the ability of any political entrepreneur to take political advantage of an oversized public program, such as public pensions, by more accurately stating the costs and benefits to voters.

The second public choice insight that explains the failure to converge toward optimal decision-making, especially when it comes to public pensions, is the ability for policymakers to push costs into the future (Buchanan and Wagner 1977[2000]; Eusepi and Wagner 2017), which minimizes voter resistance to the program. It may actually increase voter support for the program given that it enables them to reap the benefit of the program without having to shoulder the costs. This would especially be true of taxpayers, such as the wealthy, currently paying the majority of taxes to support government programs. They may even avoid future taxes for the program if they plan on retiring (and thus having lower taxable income) or intend to move to a different city or state (Inman 1981 & 1982; Sneed and Sneed 1997).

This second public choice factor can only be truly operative if Ricardian equivalence – where voters see tax-financing and debt-financing as equivalent –

---

[6] In regard to public pensions, a more generous public pension increases the competition and thus costs of securing a public employee position. Thus, even if the benefits of public employment are capitalized by the increased upfront costs of securing a job, a decrease in benefits would harm the public employee.

[7] This is even true of emergency programs designed to address a specific, temporary crisis (Higgs 1987).

does not hold. If Ricardian equivalence holds, then a political entrepreneur could gain electoral support for more accurately stating the costs of the project. Ricardian equivalence, however, doesn't hold in the presence of fiscal illusion (Eusepi and Wagner 2017, pp. 14-17). On average, we do owe our debt to ourselves, so the average level of debt appears not to matter. But, individuals do, in fact, face different circumstances. Individuals currently paying the majority of taxes are more likely to support, or at least tolerate, a program if they know that these costs will fall on unspecified future taxpayers (Eusepi and Wagner 2017), meaning different outcomes are possible when debt is used to finance a public project rather than current taxes.

Both of these public choice factors encourage an oversized public sector. When it comes to public pensions, both insights provide a theoretical explanation for sustained fiscal illusion when it comes to public pensions. This would suggest a tendency toward generosity in pension structures and benefit levels above what voters would be willing to support if they had a more accurate assessment of their costs.

This is, in fact, what we do see. Public sector employees are highly organized and effective special interest groups (Anzia and Moe 2015, 2017 & 2019; Wagner and Elder 2021). The evidence strongly suggests that pension underfunding is exacerbated by public employee unionism (Johnson 1997; Marks et al. 1988; Mitchell and Smith 1994; Wagner and Elder 2021). The support or fierce opposition of public employee unions can make or break a policymaker's chances of obtaining office. Even on basic reforms on non-pension-related issues with strong support from voters, it is difficult for policymakers to overcome opposition from public employees: for example, the inherent difficulty policymakers have had reforming policing (DeAngelis 2018; Fisk and Richardson 2017) and education (Moe 2011) in the United States, despite strong support from voters on both the left and the right for reform. When it comes to legislation affecting pensions, public employees are particularly intense and well coordinated.

Policymakers have abundant opportunities to take advantage of opportunistic accounting to misrepresent the costs of public pensions to voters (Kaspar 2011; Stalebrink 2014; Thornburg and Roasacker 2018). We will discuss many of these opportunities in more detail in Section 4, but some discussion here is warranted for demonstration purposes. For instance, pension plan contribution policy can be influenced by actuarial and accounting manipulation, increasing risk-taking in investments, and/or reducing or skipping regular contributions (Randazzo 2017). More specifically, measuring plan liabilities and assets can be manipulated by altering the actuarial assumptions regarding the discount rate to value plan liabilities, amortization schedules, the selection of mortality tables, salary growth assumptions, and/or asset smoothing.

Opportunistic accounting is feasible because, contrary to the practice of private sector defined-benefit plans, public plans in the United States do not use fair-value accounting to report pension liabilities (Easterday and Eaton 2012). Instead, they are given far greater latitude in government accounting standards to select discount rates based on expected asset returns. These misrepresentations end up also affecting the incentives of pension administrators. For instance, by discounting liabilities with the expected asset return rate, administrators have the incentive to incur greater investment risk in their portfolios in order to inflate their discount rate. A higher discount rate serves to lower their reported liabilities.

Since the 1980s, defined-benefit plans have gradually shifted from portfolios consisting largely of government securities to portfolios heavily invested in higher-risk, higher-return equities and alternatives, a trend also prompted by changes to pension plans governance as we discuss in Section 3 (The Pew Charitable Trusts and the John Arnold Foundation 2014). Valuing guaranteed pension benefits based on high-risk investment returns, by keeping the present value of plan liabilities and current-period employee and employer contribution low, enables policymakers to push costs in an obfuscated manner onto unspecified individuals in the future.

In addition to the incentive to take on investment risk in the asset portfolio in order to keep contributions low, the annual employer contribution is often subject to the discretion of the sponsor. The annual pension contribution consists of two components: the return on pension investments and a regular contribution from the employee and the employer. The investment component of the contribution is subject to some degree of volatility depending on the performance of the plan's asset portfolio.

Employee contributions are generally stable as they are typically set in negotiations with employees and deducted automatically from payroll on a regular basis.[8] Absent a constitutional or statutory provision that mandates the annual employer contribution, a sponsoring government may, however, elect to reduce or skip the employer's contributions to the plan. And, they often do. Gorina (2018), for example, finds that state plan contributions are influenced by fiscal stress, voter preferences for increased service, collective bargaining, pension board characteristics, and legislative professionalism.

---

[8] Alabama offers a recent example of employee contributions being changed. Members of the Teacher Retirement System and the Employee Retirement System in the Retirement Systems of Alabama saw their contribution rates rise from 5 percent to 7.5 percent (Dove and Smith 2016, p. 25).

Revenue structure may also play a role in affecting employer contributions at the local level, compounding the effects of fiscal illusion. A greater reliance on volatile sources of revenue, such as fees, sales, and income taxes, or increased reliance on intergovernmental transfers, may lead sponsors to underfund pensions in periods of low revenue, increasing unfunded liabilities (Gorina 2018).

Undervaluation of pension liabilities, volatile asset performance, and systematic under-contribution from the sponsor all serve to increase plan costs. These unspecified costs *will* fall on some combination of taxpayers in the form of higher taxes, citizens in the form of reduced government services, and/or public pension retirees receiving reduced benefits.

These avenues for mispresenting the financial health of public pensions are enabled by the fact that taxpayers largely do not have an adequate understanding of pension liabilities (Epple and Schipper 1981). Understanding actuarial accounting – even among investors (Picconi 2006), pension board members (Clark et al. 2006), and public employees (Mitchell 1988; Starr-McCluer and Sunden 1999) – even without the use of misleading reporting, is inherently difficult. Given the uncertainty of who the costs of underfunded pensions will fall on, as well as the complexity of actuarial reporting, means that few taxpayers will be drawn to a political entrepreneur attempting to accurately state these costs. This is especially true given the full array of other pressing political issues that will hold more prominence for voters than public pensions.

Public employees seemingly are the only group who would have the incentive to avoid the fiscal illusion and better understand the true costs and benefits of a public pension system. But, as mentioned, the evidence suggests that even public employees lack an adequate understanding of basic public finance. The incentive to dispel the illusions is also curbed due to the fact that cutting pension benefits substantially, if at all, is a very unlikely option even if pensions are underfunded. This is because pension benefits to public employees are legally or even constitutionally protected by many state governments (Giertz and Papke 2007; Monahan 2010; The Pew Charitable Trusts 2019a). In fact, because of this guarantee, public employees may even have the incentive to be implicit in understating pension costs, so as to maximize their opportunity to secure even further pension benefit increases or current salary increases (Anzia and Moe 2019; Bahl and Jump 1974; Bleakney 1973). They may also be secure in the proven effectiveness of their lobbying power, even as retirees, to ensure that any future funding shortfalls fall on the backs of taxpayers or citizens (receiving reduced government services) rather than in the form of a reduction in retirement benefits.

Given that public pensions in the United States both have entrenched special interest groups invested in protecting their privileges and are structured in a manner that enables costs to be pushed to the future, the fiscal illusion that generated the underfunded pension crisis is both a stable and expected outcome. For instance, Bagchi (2019) finds that as political competition among municipal governments increases, politicians vie for electoral support by offering increasingly more generous pension benefits and pushing costs into the future, a strategy that, of course, depends on the degree to which voters are informed about pension underfunding (Bagchi 2019). Wagner and Elder (2021) find that state teachers' unions receive a return of nearly 1,500 percent on campaign contributions in the form of increased pension generosity.

Without institutional reform, many state and local governments will remain in this equilibrium. As Oates (1988, p. 67–68) notes, however, fiscal illusions "can only operate over a limited range" due to the fact that fiscal illusions become increasingly more difficult to hide as inevitable reckonings draw near. These days of reckoning can be forced on a government earlier than anticipated during an economic downturn, when the rising share of expenditures going to support underfunded pension promises becomes obvious and painful.

When reality does set in, state and local governments will need to raise taxes, reduce government services, lower benefits, or, secure a federal bailout. This creates a moral hazard (Pauly 1968), introducing another reason to expect overpromised and underfunded public pensions, at least as currently structured in the United States, to be a stable equilibrium.[9] If a bailout can be reasonably expected, perhaps justified during an economic downturn, than state and local governments have less incentive to properly fund their pensions in anticipation of a bailout.

Public pension experts, however, have not been fooled by the fiscal illusion, as evidenced by the strong consensus among economists and finance experts that public pensions are underfunded (IGM Forum 2012; Novy-Marx and Rauh 2009; Ricketts and Walker 2012). The Financial Crisis heightened awareness of state and local governments' indebtedness in the form of both bonded, or

---

[9] Once a federal bailout is executed, and thus in the range of political possibilities, state and local policymakers will have even less incentive to reform public pensions. The recent request of a federal bailout of state governments, to address the impact of COVID-19 with an unrestricted federal bailout, or, in the case of Illinois, an explicit request for support for their underfunded pension systems, demonstrates that states with poorly funded public pensions will have the incentive to leverage crises to pursue bailouts (Walsh 2020). The European Debt Crisis provides a vivid modern example of how the moral hazard of bailouts reduces the incentives for needed reforms.

"explicit debt," and unfunded pension obligations, or "implicit debt," leading to increases in municipal debt yields in the period after the crisis (Lekniūtė et al. 2019, p. 30).[10] There are also a wide variety of reputable think tanks and nonprofits that have condensed the academic research on public pension underfunding into policy papers, popular publications, and model legislation. Credit markets have also provided signals to governments. Yet, there are few instances where state and local governments have voluntarily undertaken comprehensive reforms.[11] This raises the question of why experts have failed to impact policy debates on this pressing issue?

We believe the explanation for expert failure can also be explained by referring again to Figure 1. Experts are effective in correcting beliefs toward accuracy only under two conditions. One, is when they go directly to the public and convince a significant percentage of the electorate that they are under an illusion. This can be referred to as shifting the Overton Window – a range of ideas feasible to the electorate in the current political climate – toward a more accurate set of beliefs that was previously beyond the range of realistically available policies (Russell 2006). When it comes to public pensions, however, the complexity of pension finance makes shifting the Overton Window a difficult task.

The second opportunity for experts to help correct beliefs is when political entrepreneurs spot an electorally favorable opportunity to expose an inaccurate belief held by the public. The expert can thus be "used" by the policymaker for political advantage, that is, to move policy in a favorable direction. With public pensions having both entrenched special interest groups and the ability to pass along costs to future generations, there is little electoral incentive, and even a strong disincentive (to avoid public employee backlash), for any politician to attempt to reform inaccurate beliefs. In fact, even scholars bringing academic research to bear on state and local pension underfunding problems, have received considerable backlash from entrenched special interest groups (Bronner 2015; Costrell 2012b). There is some evidence to indicate, however, that the electoral cost of pension reforms is lower in countries with higher levels of financial literacy (Fornero and Lo Prete 2019).

Public pensions are a nonissue for most taxpayers, but one of the most important issues to outspoken, and well-organized, public employees. Thus,

---

[10] The effect of increased debt on municipal yields is stronger for explicit debt than for implicit debt. This may be because of the difference in the timing of payments between explicit and implicit debt, and investors may view governments as more likely to default on by pensions than on municipal bonds (Lekniūtė et al. 2019, p. 30–31).

[11] In Section 5 we discuss some examples of successful reforms.

even with strong expert consensus on the pressing issue of underfunded public pensions, within the current structure of public pensions, we can expect the fiscal illusion to persist.

3 The Governance of Public Pensions

Who is responsible for public pensions? That is a surprisingly difficult question to answer. Public sector pensions exist within a complex institutional environment (Matkin et al. 2019, p. 99) comprised of different spheres of governance. These include (1) stakeholders – including sponsoring governments, plan beneficiaries, and voters/taxpayers who bear the financial and fiscal risk of plan mismanagement; (2) decision makers – including boards of control, CEOs, and investment advisors to whom governments delegate plan oversight, management, and investment policies; and (3) technical experts – including actuaries, accountants, and standards-setting bodies who bring expertise and advice to bear on plan management and stewardship.

These actors help shape the institutional framework – the formal rules, laws, policies, and practices that affect pension fund performance by structuring incentives and the flow of information (Boettke et al. 2005; North 1990). Within the context of pensions, institutions create incentives, interactions, and feedback loops that can lead to a variety of possible outcomes for plan performance. The formal design of public pension institutions is shaped by external forces and signals, including the economic, political, managerial, financial, professional, and legal environment in which public pensions operate (Matkin et al. 2019, pp. 99–101). Courts also play a role in the pension governance framework, interpreting and enforcing pension legislation and contributing to the development of case law on the protections afforded to employee benefits under contract law, property rights, and gratuity approaches (Monahan 2012, p. 1035). Given all of these dimensions, it is not surprising that there is a great deal of heterogeneity in the governance structure and investment strategy among state and local pension plans (Useem and Mitchell 2000, p. 490; see also Miller and Funston 2014).

In this section we analyze some of the primary factors influencing the institutional framework of public pensions. We also describe the role and relationship of pension plan stakeholders, decision makers, and experts in fund performance and detail the knowledge and incentive problems they often face.

3.1 Stakeholders: Elected Officials, Beneficiaries, and Voters/Taxpayers

There are three primary stakeholders of public sector pension plans: (1) sponsoring governments represented by elected officials, legislators, governors, treasurers, mayors, and city officials; (2) beneficiaries (employees and retirees); and (3) voters/taxpayers (Hess and Impavido 2004, p. 58). Additional stakeholders may include capital markets participants, ratings agencies, taxpayer watchdog groups, and professional associations (Matkin et al. 2019, p. 12).

Elected officials and legislators assigned to committees that deal with employee compensation and benefits are ultimately responsible for the meta-rules governing pensions: the statutory and constitutional provisions surrounding pension benefits.[12] These meta-rules emerge in extra-legislative and legislative settings: negotiations between public sector unions and sponsoring governments, court decisions, constitutional conventions, legislative hearings, public feedback venues, and lobbying efforts. Pension-related statutes may include specific rules on plan design such as benefit formulas and eligibility criteria, protections for employee benefits, contribution and funding policies, plan governance structure, and the development of investment strategy according to environmental, social, or governance (ESG) goals (National Conference of State Legislatures 2020).

One area of particular importance for pension plan governance is the degree to which promised benefits are legally protected for employees. Especially under the threat of bankruptcy, the degree of legal protection is significant since pension promises will contend with other stakeholders, such as bondholders and taxpayers, for remedy (Skeel 2016). The degree of legal protection also influences the incentives of stakeholders.

According to The Pew Charitable Trusts (2019a, pp. 2–3), twenty-six states rely on case law or a "common-law contractual approach" in determining benefit protections. Pension benefits are protected by state constitution in eight states and by statute in six states. Five states rely on a combination of statute and judicial decision (one state relies solely on judicial decision). Indiana and statewide plans in Texas rely on gratuity (nonstatewide plans in Texas rely on the state constitution) (Selby 2011, pp. 1238–1240). Connecticut relies on a combination of property law and contract law and Minnesota relies on promissory estoppel.

Legal provisions vary in terms of the scope and degree of protection afforded to benefits. All states protect accrued benefits for employees but differ on how they define the accrual period. Twenty-three states partially or completely protect employees' unearned or future benefits (The Pew Charitable Trusts 2019a, pp. 5–6). In addition to the basic benefit, eight states provide legal

---

[12] At least five state public pensions have an independent pension commission that reports to the legislative committee as well (Peng 2009, p. 105).

protections for Cost of Living Adjustments (COLA) (The Pew Charitable Trusts 2019a, p. 6).

These legal approaches have come under increasing scrutiny where they are interpreted by courts to prevent legislatures from reducing current or future benefit accruals for employees without complementary rules or enforcement mechanisms requiring regular and sufficient funding (Monahan 2010 & 2015). Eleven states have adopted the legal precedent set by the "California rule," which holds that state statutes for retirement benefits create a contract between the employee and sponsoring government on the first day of employment and as such may not be impaired, even prospectively (Monahan 2012, p. 1032).[13]

Within this statutory/constitutional framework, elected officials influence pension fund performance in at least four important capacities. First, is the annual funding allotment going to public pensions vis-à-vis other public funding needs (Matkin et al. 2019, p. 99). For instance, elected officials can decide whether to allocate the annual required contribution (ARC), as determined by the Governmental Accounting Standards Board (GASB), or not (Matkin et al. 2019, p. 104).[14] Funding the ARC is an important factor in the funding health of public pensions (Munnell et al. 2008). The calculation of the ARC, however, is subject to manipulation depending on actuarial practice and the application of GASB guide lines. That is, even if elected officials contribute the ARC as calculated by plan actuaries, that amount may be insufficient to ensure full funding (The Pew Charitable Trusts 2015). Elected officials may reduce or shirk on the annual contribution when it competes with balancing the budget and other spending initiatives (Monahan 2015, p. 120). Meeting the annual contribution is especially susceptible to shirking during times of fiscal stress (Mitchell and Hsin 1997, p. 19). This was certainly the case for many public pensions during the Financial Crisis (Munnell et al. 2011). Even if officials increase pension funding during times of fiscal stress, it may not be enough to address the shortfall (Triest and Zhao 2014).

A lack of contribution discipline on the part of elected officials has led some states to institute statutory or constitutional provisions requiring a certain level of annual funding (Monahan 2015, p. 120). These

---

[13] Monahan (2012, p. 1032) notes the California rule, "runs contrary to the well-established legal presumption that statutes do not create contractual rights absent clear and unambiguous evidence that the legislature intended to bind itself."

[14] GASB 67/68 now adopt the language of "actuarially defined contribution" to distinguished the contribution that is contractually required versus what is determined according to professional actuarial practice.

requirements, similar to state balanced budget or tax and expenditure limits (Mitchell and Tuszynski 2012), are structurally sensitive, and thus often are not effective at improving plan health (Monahan 2015, p. 130). Statutory requirements like this are easily evaded by officials; likewise, constitutional funding provisions do not fare any better as a funding enforcement mechanism (Monahan 2015, pp. 146–147). It is difficult, though not impossible, to create clear, enforceable funding requirements that bind legislators to annually fund pensions. This is because courts cannot generally compel legislatures to appropriate funds, where those spending items are subject to legislative approval (Monahan 2015, p. 152).

The second capacity in which elected officials affect pension fund performance is through their capacity to serve directly as ex officio members on boards of control, or, to have a say in who is appointed to serve on those boards. More fundamentally, they can help determine how many members boards of control have and how each member is selected. Boards are often comprised of a mixture of both political appointees and plan participants, which can influence the types of knowledge and incentive problems faced by the board and plan administrators.[15]

Third, elected politicians also can influence fund performance by determining the degree of autonomy granted to the boards of control when it comes to making investment and other decisions (Matkin et al. 2019, p. 104). Boards can be given specific operating constraints, structural checks and balances, or other operating procedures that influence system performance. It is important to note that federal laws governing private pension plans, such as the Employee Retirement Income Security Act (ERISA), do not apply to public pensions (Peng 2009, ch. 4).[16] Thus, the discretionary authority granted by policymakers to boards of control can either enable or curtail the utilization of politically opportunistic accounting practices (Anenson 2016; Schneider and Damanpour 2001, p. 553).

The fourth way in which elected officials influence fund performance is through their ability to legislate reforms to public pensions (Peng 2009, p. 88). These reforms can range from modest, such as reporting transparency,

---

[15] David Bronner, the CEO of the Retirement Systems of Alabama, for instance, acknowledges that having 80 percent of the Teacher's Retirement System board elected by participants of the system has helped him evade the accountability of state-elected officials (Vock and Farmer 2016).

[16] Governmental pension plans were specifically excluded from ERISA due to the fact that "Adopting a funding standard similar to that required by ERISA would require many of these governments to raise their contributions by more than 100 percent, and a few by more than 400 percent" (Peng 2009, p. 88).

to major reforms, such as moving from a defined-benefit to a defined-contribution model for new employees.[17] Depending on the statutory or constitutional framework and any legal precedent, of course, elected officials may have little room to modify defined-benefit formulas for current employees.

Elected officials face both knowledge and incentive problems when it comes to exercising their influence over public pensions. The knowledge problems emerge because policymakers often do not have sufficient expertise to understand the intricacies of public pension accounting, especially in a sophisticated enough manner relative to plan administrators, lobbyists, and experts. This is aggravated by the fact that most states do not have full-time legislators (National Conference on State Legislators 2017). Thus, they lack the knowledge to parse through information presented by different stakeholders, such as boards of control, CEOs, public employees, and lobbyists, which often come to conflicting assessments and recommendations on annual contributions, funded health, investment policy, or possible reforms.

Elected officials also face two primary incentive problems when it comes to their responsibility and authority to oversee public pensions. First, they may have more pressing or politically prominent policy issues. So even if they had the wherewithal to comprehend actuarial reports and assess the funding health of the plan, they often lack the time and political incentive to do so. This is especially true when state or local governments are facing fiscal stress or operating under operative balanced budget constraints. Limited finances can lead to pensions becoming underfunded since policymakers prioritize spending on the most politically opportunistic projects (Chaney et al. 2002; Eaton and Nofsinger 2004; Mitchell and Smith 1994). Even during normal times, politicians are apt to fund more prominent and electorally beneficial projects rather than address more distanced and less prominent problems, as we saw with the levies in New Orleans prior to Hurricane Katrina (Boettke and Smith 2010) and the lead water-pipe crisis still facing many American cities (Troesken 2006). This is especially the case if there is the possibility of federal funds (or a federal bailout), as with state and local infrastructure repair (Gribbin 2019). Very few voters, for instance, understand or are concerned about the underfunding of pensions, making solving the problem a very low-priority political issue for many policymakers.

---

[17] As mentioned, even elected officials typically cannot modify promises, or even promises of future benefits, made to current employees and retirees (Peng 2009, p. 89).

The second incentive problem they face is that, to get elected or re-elected, policymakers make promises to provide concentrated benefits to key interest groups and to disperse the costs among taxpayers (Hess and Squire 2010, p. 590; Olson 1965). Some of the most active and organized special interest groups, of course, are public employees. This is especially true when they are unionized (Anzia and Moe 2015, 2017 & 2019; Marks et al. 1988; Mitchell and Smith 1994; Johnson 1997). When it comes to public pensions, policymakers have the option to not just disperse the costs among current taxpayers, but to use "politically opportunistic" accounting to hide the true costs of public pension promises and even push expenses into the future (Stalebrink 2014; also see Hall and Hovey 1980; Inman 1981 & 1982; Kasper 2011). Wagner and Elder (2021), for instance, find that teachers' unions are able to use their political clout, especially campaign contributions, to secure larger retirements by pushing the costs onto future taxpayers. While solving the pension-underfunding problem is a low priority item for voters, maintaining existing pension benefits, and even expanding them, is a high priority item for public employees. Public employees have the organizational power to reward policymakers who deliver favorable policy and to punish policymakers who attempt to reform public pensions.

Elected officials also have a strong incentive to cater to another special interest group – businesses. Policymakers would prefer to see public pension investments directed to opportunities within the state. Factory expansions and hiring expansions within the state make great photo opportunities, create loyal voting supporters, and generate campaign donations. Even better if these in-state investments can be directed in an electorally strategic way. In fact, the evidence suggests that policymakers have such a strong incentive to cater to in-state businesses via public pension portfolios that they often do so at the cost of substantial loss of investment return (Bradley et al. 2016; Brown et al. 2015; Hochberg and Rauh 2013).

Sponsoring governments risk creditworthiness and policymaker's voter dissatisfaction, of course, if a plan is extremely mismanaged (beyond what even opportunistic accounting can cover up) or facing insolvency. Pension beneficiaries and current and future taxpayers are, after all, the residual claimants of the plan. They bear the financial risk if government sponsors shirk on annual contributions or fail in their oversight of the plan's investment strategy. Depending on the degree to which a plan is underfunded, beneficiaries may be expected to accept reductions in benefit accruals and payouts while taxpayers may face higher taxes or reduced services to meet promised obligations to retirees. Nevertheless, with their constitutional or legal protections and lobbying power, public employees may bank on the fact that they will be able to organize against and block any attempts at reducing retirement benefits in the future.

3.2 Decision makers: Boards of Control, CEOs, and Investment Advisors

While governments and elected officials are ultimately accountable to pension beneficiaries and taxpayers for the statutory/constitutional framework and fiscal health of pension plans, the practical aspects of plan governance including oversight, accountability, transparency, and the management of plans is delegated to various internal decision makers (Stalebrink 2017).

Boards of control are the group directly entrusted with the governance policy of public pensions. Boards of control are commonly granted the explicit authority by policymakers to determine the investments, investment managers, benefits, actuarial assumptions, and asset allocation policies of a public pension (Hess 2005, p. 194; Mitchell et al. 2001; Mitchell and Hsin 1997; Peng 2009, p. 95–96; Zorn 1997). They often also hold the authority to appoint and monitor executives within the pension system (Anenson 2016, p. 277). They can also determine the degree to which they delegate their authority to pension administrators.

Boards of control of state and local public pensions in the United States are organized in four different governance structures (Miller and Funston 2014). Some public pensions have one board of control overseeing the investment and administrative functions of the plan under one CEO. Other councils have separate boards of controls and CEOs for their separate investment and administrative functions. Some have separate investment and administration functions and CEOs but under the same board of control. Finally, a handful of public pensions have sole fiduciary (no board of control) oversight of both their investment and administration functions.

Public pension boards of control are typically comprised of a diverse range of members. Some board members are either politically appointed or serve as ex officio members due to their elected or appointed government position (for instance, it is common for a state governor, comptroller, or treasurer to serve ex officio on a board of control). Both retired and active employees often elect some of their fellow plan participants to dedicated board positions. Finally, some boards have positions for members of the general public. These boards of controls can have a measurable impact on public pension funding health (Wang and Peng 2016). The extent of their influence, however, is controlled by the degree of autonomy granted to the board of control by elected officials (DiSalvo 2018, p. 6), as well as the varying legal fiduciary responsibilities set forth by each state (Anenson 2016).

The composition of these boards, in particular, can impact public pension performance given the knowledge and incentive problems they create (Anenson

2016, p. 275; Dove et al. 2018). For instance, appointed or ex officio members are, as professionals, likely to have the most knowledge of pension accounting and finance. But, they likely also have the pressure to administer the public pension in a manner that elevates political expediency, or even rewards political contributions, compared to long-run funding health (Andonov et al. 2018; Hess 2005, p. 197). This can be driven both by loyalty to the politicians (or party) that appointed them and a desire to leverage the position to advance their own political careers (Hess 2005, p. 197).

Appointed and ex officio members may also face pressure to direct plan assets into in-state investments, compromising plan objectives in pursuit of investments that will generate economic development rather than maximize returns. These types of in-state investments often underperform other investment categories (Bradley et al. 2016; Coronado et al. 2003; Hochberg and Rauh 2013; Useem and Mitchell 2000).[18] And, in-state investments are often steered by ex officio board members toward politically motivated projects (Bradley et al. 2016; Brown et al. 2015).

Appointed or ex officio members may also prioritize investing in socially responsible firms over maximizing returns (Aubry et al. 2020; Hoepner and Schopohl 2019; Marlowe 2014; Munnell and Chen 2016; Munnell and Sundén 2001). In fact, some encourage public pensions to embrace their status as major institutional investors to push through a range of minor and major reforms on corporations (Clark and Hebb 2004; Coffee, Jr. 1991; Hess 2005).[19]

There may be differences between even ex officio and appointed members. For instance, ex officio board members may prefer less risky portfolios than appointed members (Dobra and Lubich, 2013, p. 98).

Plans members, relative to appointed and ex-officio members, often have even less familiarity with the finance and pension accounting concepts necessary to make informed decisions (Andonov et al. 2018; Dove et al. 2018). In addition, knowing their pension benefits are legally or constitutionally secure (Forman 2009, p. 129–131; Peng 2009, ch. 4.2; The Pew Charitable Trusts 2019a), plan members may have an incentive to be complicit in the underreporting of plan costs to make it more politically viable to expand benefits, cost of living adjustments, budgets, bureaucracies, or even current compensation

---

[18] In an unpublished working paper, Brown et al. (2015) find that the in-state investments of state public pensions do generate excess returns, but that these investments are often politically motivated.

[19] Smythe et al. (2015) note that the California Public Employees Retirement System (CalPERS) is a pioneer in shareholder activism and has included it as part of its investment goals since 1987.

(Anzia and Moe 2019; Bahl and Jump 1974; Bleakney 1973; Johnson 1997; Marks et al. 1988; Mitchell and Smith 1994; Sneed and Sneed 1997).[20]

Some evidence shows that even retired and active board members differ in their investment preferences. Plans dominated by retired members, for instance, tend to have higher levels of investment in alternatives and equities (Dobra and Lubich 2013, p. 95). There may even be differences in preferences among active state employees, depending on their expected tenure on the job (Costrell 2018). Early leavers, such as military spouses and untenured professors, receive far less in benefits than career employees, and are far less likely than career employees to be represented on a board.

Board composition and size may also influence investment and portfolio risk tolerance. For instance, larger boards are correlated with riskier investment portfolios (Dobra and Lubich 2013, p. 98). Additional research shows that states with strong unions tend to use higher discount rates to obscure the burden of plan liabilities in reporting (Bosnall et al. 2019, p. 1331).

3.3 Pension CEOs and Bureaucrats

Day-to-day administration of public pensions is undertaken by bureaucracies working in city and state public pensions across the nation. Depending on the size of the retirement system, this includes a CEO overseeing both operational and investment teams. While pension plan bureaucrats – especially upper management and those on the investment or accounting teams – are often very knowledgeable stakeholders regarding pension accounting and finance, they face a host of incentive problems inherent to bureaucracies, including budget-maximization, self-preservation, inertia, and groupthink (Niskanen 1968; Tullock 2005). Those employed at public pensions, after all, have a strong interest in preserving the system. Depending on the composition of the board, their continued employment often depends on pleasing the majority of the board members.[21] Thus, the classic information asymmetry problem, where one party holds more information than the other, and thus faces an incentive to exploit that information asymmetry, emerges (Akerlof 1970).

Given the number of dollars at play, it is not surprising that pensions, both public and private, face additional incentive problems for strategic and opportunistic behavior when it comes to investing (Anenson 2016; Muir

---

[20] Labor unions, after all, opposed the Employee Retirement Income Security Act of 1974, which mandated transparency and uniform standards for private pension plans (Wooten 2005, p. 204). Leaders of the unions knew, rightfully so, that more transparent accounting would undermine support for defined-benefit retirement plans among corporate executives and shareholders.

[21] See, for instance, Vock and Farmer (2016).

2016).[22] Setting investment strategy is a function that may be assumed by the board of trustees or delegated to board investment committees or professional managers who may either be employed with the pension plan or contracted externally.[23]

The rules surrounding pension investments have changed over time, giving trustees and investors greater discretion in shaping asset portfolios. Beginning in the 1980s, public sector pensions, influenced by modern portfolio theory (MPT), moved away from selecting investments from 'legal lists' that generally limited pensions to investing primarily in bonds to a prudent person standard in making investment selections. The Pew Charitable Trusts and Laura and John Arnold Foundation (2014) released a study finding that in 1952 public pensions portfolios consisted of 96 percent fixed income and cash. By 1992 this fell to 47 percent and by 2012 to 27 percent, with the majority of investments concentrated in equities and alternatives (The Pew Charitable Trusts and Laura and John Arnold Foundation 2014, p. 3). In the last decade, pension plans have continued to shift their investments into higher-risk categories in pursuit of higher returns.[24] Ivashina and Lerner (2018), for instance, find a large shift toward alternative investments following the Financial Crisis.

A few states continue to fix the percentage of pension investments dedicated to hedge funds and private equity, though even these have been gradually relaxed to allow for greater investor discretion (Rose and Seligman 2013, pp. 5–6). The prudent-person rule may create a herding effect as pension officials seek to insulate themselves from criticism from legislators and plan beneficiaries. Herding may also arise where trustees or officials hire consultants offering standard investment advice (Rose and Seligman 2013, p. 6). Plan officials may also herd when investing in alternatives since these investments tend to provide less information on performance and measured volatility (Rose and Seligman 2013, p. 6).[25]

While studies indicate that investment returns are not affected by whether the plan relies on in-house or external investment managers (Mitchell and Hsin 1997, p. 16), there is a risk that the selection of managers, and the pay they

---

[22] Private pensions, even under union influence, were not immune to this type of pressure (Wehrwein 1964, p. 1).

[23] Internal governance procedures don't always operate as intended. For instance, until rule changes were implemented in 2013, the CEO of the Retirement Systems of Alabama, David Bronner, "sidestepped the [investment] committee by securing proxy votes from two out of the committee's three members" (Vock and Farmer 2016).

[24] According to the Public Plans Database in 2018, public pension plans held 74 percent of their investments in riskier categories including stocks, alternatives, commodities, and real estate. See Biggs and Norcross (2020).

[25] The similar lack of transparency in the construction industry makes it an area of public spending that is particularly susceptible to corruption (Chan and Owusu 2017).

receive, may be influenced by political considerations (Dyck et al. 2019). Begenau and Siriwardane (2020), using data from 1990 to 2018, find that, based upon plan characteristics such as committee size, pension size, relationship with investment managers, and governance structure, some public pensions systematically paid more in fees to the *same* investment manager than other public pension systems.[26] Overall, in pursuit of higher returns, many public pensions have resorted to investing with hedge funds and private equity firms at management fees up to 2 percent plus up to 20 percent of gains (Morgenson 2017).

The Government Financial Officers Associations (GFOA) has produced policy guidance stressing the need for a merit-based approach in hiring investment managers for public pensions. This guideline was tested in 2003 when the Ohio legislature introduced a bill that would have required the state to direct 50 to 70 percent of its investments to Ohio-based companies. The measure was opposed by the state's pension administrators and professional groups and highlights the temptation for elected officials to influence the investment practices and decisions of pension administrators (Coggburn and Riddick 2007, p. 1005).

Pension administrators and managers may also be pressured in times of fiscal stress to achieve high returns in order to keep contributions low. Over time, pension portfolios have increased in both risk and in the diversification of asset classes (Coggburn and Riddick 2007, p. 1004; Novy-Marx and Rauh 2009). Accounting standards have also played a role in incentivizing greater investment risk in pension portfolios, which we review in greater detail in Section 4.

Even when pensions are well funded, pension CEOs may worry about the risk of policymakers reducing benefits for members or reducing contributions. This has served as the basis for many public pension administrators arguing for targeting an 80 percent funded ratio, because a well-funded pension becomes a lucrative source of funds to policymakers, who may be tempted to reduce funding going forward or to exert additional political influence on how the funds are invested (Lawson 2012). An *Issue Brief* from the American Academy of Actuaries (2012), however, calls the 80 percent target a myth and argues that public pension plans should have 100 percent funding as their objective.

3.4 Technical Experts: Accounting and Actuarial Professionals, Standards-Setting Bodies

The accounting and actuarial professions also have governance roles over public pensions.[27] This influence comes in two primary capacities:

---

[26] See also Andonov et al. (2018).

[27] For a more in-depth treatment of the role of accounting and actuary professionals, see Section 4.

determination of actuarial assumptions, and determination of the level of transparency and clarity used in pension reporting. As experts, the accounting and actuarial professions often have the most accurate knowledge of pension accounting. But, as with other professions – such as the Federal Reserve (Fabo et al. 2020; Epstein and Carrick-Hagenbarth 2011; White 2005), who suffer from groupthink and status quo bias – advancements may be rejected under pressure for conformity and tradition. For instance, both private and public pension actuaries have been reluctant to incorporate established prudent financial practices from economics and finance (Bader and Gold 2003; Exley et al. 1997; Gold 2003; Waring 2012). Accountants and actuaries have also resisted pressure to make public pension accounting and reporting more transparent and accessible to policymakers and taxpayers (Thornburg and Rosacker 2018). One reason for this may be the hope that favorable markets (beyond reasonable expectation) will generate the returns necessary to shore up these funds without having to face the embarrassment of admitting that their traditional accounting methods inadequately informed policymakers and the public (Waring 2012, p. 224). A United States Senate report on the first decade of the ERISA (U.S. Senate 1984), for instance, notes that "full disclosure may lead to embarrassing reports of underperformance by political appointees. As long as the disclosure of this performance can be hidden or delayed, those responsible will not be held accountable."

Given the difficulty inherent to understanding pension financing, it is problematic that the reporting for public pensions isn't more accessible. As Thornburg and Rosacker (2018) write, "The accounting profession has failed to provide the public with understandable information by circulating pension accounting disclosures that are so complex that average taxpayers are unable to understand their meaning."

Some of these problems, however, are not directly the responsibility of the accounting and actuarial professions. One reason that public pensions lag behind even private pensions in reporting and transparency is that public pensions are not subject to the Employee Retirement Income Security Act (ERISA) of 1974 (Forman 2009). Most public pension plans, however, do voluntarily choose to follow the accounting and reporting standards set by the GASB (Forman 2009, p. 106). If public pension plans were held to the same exacting standards as private pensions, as set forth by ERISA, they would be held to be underfunded in violation of the law.

Another reason – again not the direct responsibility of the accounting and actuarial professions – is the continued use of defined-benefit models. Promising an employee a certain level of benefits from retirement to death (and, in some cases, spousal benefits), however, requires projecting life expectancy of employees ahead of time and thereby saving enough, and investing appropriately, to sustainably fund a lifetime of benefits.

Actuarial firms face several incentive problems. The handful of major firms specializing in actuarial accounting for public pensions are hired directly by the pension sponsors and thus have an incentive to, within the scope of professional practice, shine as favorable a light as possible on the plan to keep their business. The leeway in the accounting standards enables them to exercise wide discretion when it comes to this. These actuarial firms also serve as consultants and provide testimony to legislators and pension executives when they are considering pension reforms and to GASB when considering changes to accounting standards to public pensions. Recommending major changes in reporting or in the structure of public pensions, could result in the loss of their actuarial contracts (Waring 2012, p. 225). One major actuarial firm, Cavanaugh MacDonald Consulting, which has multiple state and local public pensions and healthcare clients, even received a startup loan from the Retirement Systems of Alabama (Canary 2015), creating an obvious conflict of interest for a firm serving public pension clients, especially one serving the Retirement Systems of Alabama in a no-bid contract.

3.5 Governmental Accounting Standards Board

The GASB was established in 1984 to create voluntary standards within the accounting profession for public pension accounting (Peng 2009, p. 76).[28] Of the eighty-two standards issued by GASB, eighteen concern pensions or post-employment benefits (Foltin et al. 2017, p. 1). These GASB standards on pensions offer guidance on reporting, actuarial assumptions, and cost methods. One area in which GASB has played an important role in pension accounting concerns the calculation of plan liabilities and assets, and the annual funding required to fully fund benefits.

Projecting plan assets and liabilities out into the future requires many assumptions and GASB rules allow actuarial firms to exercise considerable discretion. Until 2012, GASB authorized six different actuarial cost methods, which led to different assessments of funding health (Peng 2009, p. 61). From 1994 until 2014, plans relied on GASB 25 to measure unfunded liability and the annual required contribution. GASB 25 permits plans to use the expected return on plan assets as the discount rate to calculate the present value of the liability. A higher discount rate, such as that based on expected returns, lowers both the present value of the pension liability and the annual contribution required to fund benefits. This introduces an incentive for elected officials, plan managers,

---

[28] For a more in-depth treatment of the role of accounting and actuary professionals, see Section 4.

and actuaries to assume higher rates of return in order to raise their discount rates in order to lower annual contributions. This, thereby, creates the incentive for plans to incur more investment risk to justify high assumed rates of return (Brown and Wilcox 2009; Novy-Marx and Rauh 2009). The standard has been criticized by economists as violating financial theory and practice, a subject discussed in more detail in Section 4.

Mounting criticism of GASB 25 and GASB 27 prompted a review of these guide lines resulting in their replacement by GASB 67 and GASB 68, respectively in 2014, which introduced a hybrid approach to discount rate selection, allowing plans to select the expected rate of return on plan assets to value the funded portion of the liability, and to apply the return on a high-quality municipal bond index to value the unfunded portion of the liability. GASB undertook this reform in response to a multi-decade educational effort on the part of a small community of actuaries and financial economists attempting to address the problem with conflating the discount rate used to calculate the plan's liabilities with the expected return on plan assets (Himick and Brivot 2018, p. 34). The compromise rule, however, did not address the fundamental measurement issue, or change the incentive to manipulate discount rates to present more favorable liabilities (Weinberg and Norcross 2017).

4 Pension Accounting and Reporting

The performance of US public sector pensions is deeply connected to the measurement approaches and reporting conventions developed by actuaries, accountants, and standards-setting bodies as public sector plans expanded during the twenieth century. Through the period of the Great Recession, the techniques used by actuaries and recommended by the Actuarial Standards Board (ASB) to model pension plan costs for sponsors remained largely insulated from developments in financial economics (Bader and Gold 2003, p. 4). Similarly, accounting guide lines developed by the GASB used to produce government financial reports emerged independently from those developed for the private sector under the Financial Accounting Standards Board (FASB), leading to divergent practices in the measurement and reporting of pension plan financial condition between the private and public sectors (Flesher et al. 2019, p. 68).

The most significant consequence of the disciplinary isolation of the actuarial profession and the separation of public and private sector accounting standards is that by the mid-2000s actuarial valuations and government financial reports were understating the actual or market value of pension liabilities by trillions of dollars, leading to the underestimation of required contributions, increased risk-taking in investments, and the growth of unfunded liabilities on the balance sheets of many state and local governments. The key disconnect between the actuarial and financial economics framework involves the question of how to select the discount rate used to establish the present value of liabilities. This, in turn, provides the basis for determining the amount needed to fund liabilities and the accounting of pension benefits in government financials.

Actuarial and government accounting standards link the present value of risk-free pension liabilities to the expected return on risky assets, effectively increasing the likelihood of funding gaps due to fluctuations in the performance of plan assets. The approach came under intense scrutiny and criticism following the Financial Crisis, prompting both the ASB and GASB to modify earlier standards.

In this Section we review the key standards used in determining a funding strategy for pension plans via actuarial valuations. We also analyze how governments account for and report pension liabilities and assets in their financial statements. We discuss the theoretical and practical consequences of earlier standards on the fiscal viability of public pensions. We conclude with an overview of the recent reforms to these standards based on a decades-long critique by actuarial and financial professionals and the impact of the Financial Crisis on municipal fiscal condition and pension plan funding levels.

4.1 Measuring Pension Liabilities and Assets: Actuarial and Reporting Conventions

A defined-benefit pension represents deferred compensation. This means that the employer agrees to provide the employee regular payments in retirement based on a formula that depends on the number of years worked, final salary, and a salary replacement factor. The basic actuarial challenge is to project the value of promised benefits, calculate their present value, and then determine the contribution needed to fund them. The actuarial model is built to help the sponsor determine a funding policy. A funding policy helps to allocate costs over a period to manage annual contributions to prefund benefits while considering intergenerational equity and contribution stability for the sponsor. These goals are not necessarily mutually supporting. A policy designed to fully prefund employees' benefits in the period they are earning those benefits may reduce contribution stability and predictability for the sponsor.

The contribution required by the sponsor to adequately fund the plan is calculated on an annual basis. This calculation is influenced by several actuarial assumptions, including the discount rate used to calculate the present value of the liability, the amortization period over which the payments are stretched, the selection of the actuarial cost method, and the smoothing of fluctuations in asset values. The smoothing of asset values is the process through which investment gains and losses are gradually recognized on the books in order to keep contributions steady during market swings.

It is important to note that these four "levers" do not change the underlying value of pension liabilities and assets. They only affect their "book value." When the book value is at variance with the actual or market value of plan liabilities and assets, plans run the risk of overfunding or underfunding. Overfunding causes the misallocation of public budgetary dollars. Underfunding not only puts the health of the system at risk, it can also lead to the expansion of benefits (or the roll back of previous reforms) based on an incomplete understanding of the costs.

States facing adverse fiscal conditions tend to have a greater reliance on these discretionary assumptions when it comes to valuing their pension liabilities (Naughton et al. 2015). The Financial Crisis, however, forced many state and local public sector plans to confront the extent to which overtly optimistic assumptions obscured the true value of their liabilities. Not having an accurate grasp of their pension liabilities led to both inadequate funding and the assumption of excessive risk in their investment portfolios.

In the remainder of Section 4, we review each of these actuarial assumptions and objections to them from economists, actuaries, and financial professionals.

4.1.a The Discount Rate

The actuarial assumption with the largest impact on determining the annual contribution to fund benefits is the discount rate used to calculate the present value of the liability. This is due to two properties of discounting: (1) the discount rate and the net present value are inversely related: higher discount rates result in lower present values and vice versa; (2) the present value is also extremely sensitive to changes in the discount rate.

Actuarial practice allows for the use of the expected (but unrealized) rate of return on the plan's assets as the discount rate to value the plan's liabilities, effectively matching the value of the plan's liabilities to the expected performance of the plan's assets, an approach that predates the development of financial economics (Waring 2012, p. 21–22). As Bader and Gold (2003, p. 1) note, the traditional actuarial model "anticipates expected outcomes without reflecting the price of risk." This approach was codified into standards promulgated by the ASB in several Actuarial Standards of Practice (ASOPs) including ASOP No. 4 (ASB 2013b), ASOP No. 27 (ASB 2020), and ASOP No. 44 (ASB 2009). The approach was further reinforced by GASB for the purposes of financial reporting for state and local governments in GASB No. 25 (GASB 1994a) and GASB No. 27 (GASB 1994b).

The actuarial approach to the selection of the discount rate to value liabilities is at variance with financial economic theory and practice. Pension liabilities – a stream of future cash flows – should be discounted based on their risk and the projected timing of payments. Liabilities are independent in value from the composition of the asset portfolio used to fund them (Modigliani and Miller 1958, p. 268). Most public pension benefits are protected from impairment in state statutes or constitutions making them equivalent, or, in some cases, safer, than government debt. Public pensions thus represent a type of "implicit debt" on the balance sheets of sponsoring governments (Lekniute, Beetsma, and Ponds 2019, p. 1). This suggests the discount rate used to value pension liabilities should be based on the yield of a riskless equivalent, such as the yield on default-free government bonds (Brown and Wilcox 2009, p. 541; Novy-Marx and Rauh 2009).

There is some debate over which type of bond is best suited to valuing public pensions, as it would need to factor in the degree to which pensions are legally protected and default-free, as well as the average maturity of the liabilities. If public pensions are legally more secure than general obligation bonds, then the appropriate discount rate matches the yield on default-free, zero-coupon US Treasuries (Novy-Marx and Rauh 2011, p. 174). If there is some default risk, or if the state is as likely to default on its pensions as it is on general obligation bonds, a tax-adjusted municipal bond rate may be a better match (Novy-Marx and Rauh 2011, p. 174). Brown and Pennacchi (2016) further suggest that the rate used depends on whether you are calculating the funding value or the market value. To determine the funding value, or the amount of over- or underfunding, the default-free rate should be used. To calculate the market value, or what it would cost to sell the liability to an insurance company, the rate should accurately reflect any default risk that the sponsor may have (Brown and Pennacchi 2016, p. 255).

For many decades, the actuarial practices of using the expected return on assets as the discount rate to value liabilities did not cause much damage. This is because pension portfolios were largely invested in fixed-income assets. The rate of return on public pension portfolios represented portfolios primarily consisting of low-risk bonds, making the asset portfolio closer in risk to default-free pension liabilities (Waring 2012, p. 22)

As the return on fixed-income assets fell, pension plans began to "reach for yield" and take on higher levels of risk. They did this by investing in portfolios heavily composed of equities and an even riskier asset classification known as "alternatives" consisting of private equity, real estate, or commodities (Andonov et al. 2017, p. 2558; Brown and Wilcox 2009; Lucas and Zelders 2009; Novy-Marx and Rauh 2009). Public pension funds continue to increase the risk in their investment portfolios in response to lower funding ratios and due to the persistence of low interest rates on bonds (Lu et al. 2019, p. 3).

The continued use of the expected return on plan assets as the discount rate to value liabilities introduced a type of fiscal illusion in both actuarial valuations and financial reports, producing a trillion-dollar gap between the book value and market value of pension liabilities. Under actuarial book methods, US public sector plans were underfunded by $1.378 trillion in 2015. Using market valuation and risk-free discount rates increases the funding gap to $4.1 trillion (Rauh 2017).[29] Since 2008, public pension funds have gradually adjusted expected returns on assets downward with the average discount rate moving from 8 percent in 2008 to 7.3 percent in 2017, shrinking the risk premia assumed by plans and increasing required contribution amounts (The Pew Charitable Trusts 2019b, p. 1).

4.1.b Amortization

Actuarial amortization methods, by distributing payments over a long period, can be used by plan sponsors to ease the fiscal burden of any given plan. Long, open-amortization methods stretch payments over thirty years and reset the amortization period periodically. This keeps annual contributions at a lower level while never fully paying off the liability (Boyd and Yin 2016, p. 5). Closed amortization methods, on the other hand, pay off the liability over a defined period, typically between fifteen and thirty years.

Plans may also choose to use level dollar amortization, in which a fixed dollar amount is paid each year, or level-percent of annual payroll, which eases initial payments on the sponsor by backloading contributions as payroll rises over time. In 2013, 40 percent of a sample of public plans used open-amortization methods and 71 percent of plans used level-percent methods (Boyd and Yin 2016,p. 6). There is a tendency for plans to combine open amortization with long repayment periods (Boyd and Yin 2016, p, 6). The most conservative method, closed fifteen-year level dollar, was the most rarely used amortization method (Boyd and Yin, 2016, p. 7).

It is worth noting here that GASB rules contribute to misunderstanding when it comes to pension reform. When a pension plan closes, such as when a plan is closed to enable new members to switch to a reformed plan, GASB requires switching to level dollar methods when calculating the annual contribution.

---

[29] A 2019 update puts the total unfunded liability at $4.145 trillion (Rauh 2019).

Thus, if the system uses level-percent methods, the switch to the more conservative level dollar method gives the false sense that the transition increases costs to the sponsor (Costrell 2012a).

4.2 Actuarial Value of Assets: Asset Smoothing

Pension plans are funded from a combination of employee and employer contributions that are invested in a portfolio of assets. The return on assets varies from year to year with the potential for large swings in earnings or losses depending on the degree of investment risk in the portfolio. Asset smoothing is adopted to gradually recognize these gains or losses over a period of several years in order to avoid sharp swings in contributions.

GASB gives plan sponsors a wide range of discretion when it comes to asset smoothing, making it another lever that can be used to engage in opportunistic accounting. This is especially true during financial downturns, when asset smoothing "can be viewed as a 'denial and delay strategy'" (Chen 2018, p. 265). The proportion of public plans using asset smoothing, for instance, increased from 63 percent in 2001 to 82 percent in 2010, a period encompassing the Financial Crisis (Andonov 2014, p. 27). In addition, between 2002 and 2013, thirty-five public pension systems extended the length of their smoothing period to further spread the reporting of incurred losses (Chen 2018, p. 263). More generally, Chen (2018, p. 268) finds that each standard deviation in long-term fiscal stress increases asset smoothing by about a half-year.

Traditionally, pensions have smoothed gains and losses over a period of between three and ten years, with five-year smoothing periods being the most common (Chen 2018). Asset smoothing generates an Actuarial Value of Assets (AVA) which differs from the actual or Market Value of Assets (MVA). While the intent is to minimize the fiscal impact of large investment swings in any given year on the sponsor's budget, a necessary consequence is reporting that presents an incomplete picture of incurred losses from economic downturns to plan trustees and politicians. Asset smoothing thus conceals the impact of the investment risk undertaken by pension systems.

4.3 Actuarial Cost Method

Until recently, GASB authorized six different actuarial cost methods, which led to very different assessments of funding health (Peng 2009, p. 61). Cost methods allocate the present value of accrued benefits to different periods and may be computed, as mentioned earlier, as a percent of payroll or a level dollar amount. The selection of a cost method and computation approach can be used to push costs into the future. Boyd and Yin (2016) find that even if investment return assumptions are met every year *and* the sponsor contributes the full annual contribution, the effect of the most commonly used methods are unlikely to fully fund the plan in thirty years (Boyd and Yin 2016, p. 28).

Under newly revised standards GASB 67 (2012a) and 68 (2012b) limits governments to using only one cost method: entry age normal calculated as a level percent of payroll. The impetus for limiting actuaries to selecting one method was to ensure greater comparability among plans (GASB 2012a). The entry age normal method (EAN) allocates benefits equally over an employee's working life, thus, funding benefits as they are earned. GASB 67 (2012b) recommends the EAN method be computed as a level percent of payroll that has the feature of backloading contributions, meaning that required contributions increase as payroll increases over time.

Limiting actuaries to one cost method does not eliminate the potential for variation in how funding requirements are calculated. The major assumptions going into these cost methods, including the discount rate, the assumed salary growth rate, assumed inflation rate, decrement assumptions, asset smoothing period, and amortization period, are extremely sensitive to even small changes (Forman 2009; Matkin et al. 2019, p. 104–106; Peng 2009, ch. 3). Of all these factors, assumptions regarding the discount rate have an outsized impact on the measurement of plan liabilities (Novy-Marx and Rauh 2009).

4.4 History of Actuarial and Government Accounting Standards

The ASB sets Actuarial Standards of Practice (ASOPs) that are used to guide actuaries in their analysis. ASOPs are binding on professional actuaries but are not strongly prescriptive. Actuaries may exercise professional discretion in selecting and applying key assumptions and methods (ASB 2013a).

Importantly, ASOPs do not flow from actuarial theory or established principles (Gold 2016, p. 18). They reflect methods and practices developed by actuaries as plans grew in complexity and size in the mid-twentieth century (Waring 2012, p. 21). Technical innovations and flawed habits were embedded into formal actuarial standards without a means of testing their reliability and accuracy in light of related disciplines, including the emerging field of financial economics (Waring 2012, p. 23).

Bader and Gold (2003) note that the actuarial model successfully adapted to changes in plan governance as pensions moved from being managed by insurance companies to trustees in the 1950s and 1960s. The model also adopted some aspects of modern portfolio theory as plans began to expand asset portfolios to include equities in the 1960s and 1970s (Bader and Gold 2003, p. 1). The passage of the Employee Retirement Income Security Act of 1974 (ERISA) halted further progress for several more decades by freezing current actuarial practices into federal regulation (Bader and Gold 2003, p. 1; Waring 2012, p. 23). The result was an actuarial model "less suited to financial measurement and reporting" (Bader and Gold, 2003, p. 1) and one that was prone to misstating the value of plan liabilities and funding requirements.

The GASB also issues voluntary financial and reporting standards for state and local governments. GASB's creation in 1984 was in part due to government accountants' concern that standards issued by the FASB for the private sector would supersede those used in governments, particularly standards issued to measure pension benefits (Foltin et al. 2017, p. 60). In 1980, FASB issued its first pension standard, Statement of Financial Accounting Standards (SFAS) No. 35, which required pension plans to report the fair market value of assets (FASB 1980a). The National Conference of Government Accountants (NCGA), a "pseudo-standard setting" body for municipal governments asked FASB for several deferrals from implementing the new standard and began to lay the groundwork for a separate accounting organization (Fotlin et al. 2017, p. 60; Roybark et al. 2012).

GASB standards effectively thus avoided, first by deferrals, and then by creating a separate organization, the more demanding standards developed by FASB for the private sector. These include SFAS 87, which required companies to report pension liabilities on their balance sheets – a standard that was strongly resisted by both accounting firms and corporations as damaging to debt-to-equity ratios (Foltin et al. 2017, p. 61). SFAS 87 also recommended the use of the return on high-quality, fixed-income investments to value pension liabilities, known as the "settlement cost" or the amount it would cost to sell the obligation to an insurance company to pay out the benefits as an annuity (Naughton et al. 2015, p. 224).

By creating a separate organization, GASB delayed for decades the implementation of standards that would provide a full and accurate picture of the financial condition of pension plans offered by state and local governments. Accounting standards for pensions and other post-employment benefits made up a large part of GASB's initial agenda and continue to be an area of focus. Eighteen of the eighty-two standards issued by GASB concern pensions or post-employment benefits (Foltin et al. 2017, p. 1). The most significant standards promulgated by GASB affecting pensions – GASB 25 (1994a) and GASB 27 (1994b) – enshrined legacy actuarial practices while private sector standard setting evolved to reflect new learning and advances in financial economics. GASB 25 (1994a), for instance, recommended that the expected return on plan assets be used as the discount rate to value liabilities and permitted the practice of asset smoothing.

GASB 27 (1994b), concerning the methods to calculate the annual required contribution, codified the use of amortization assumptions to spread gains and losses into the future as an accepted practice. Additionally, GASB 27 (1994b) allowed public pensions to only report the "net pension expense" or any shortfall in the annual contribution to the plan in lieu of the total pension liability in government financial statements (Naughton et al. 2015, p. 224).

The methodological flaws and practical consequences of government actuarial and accounting practices did not go unnoticed. Beginning in the 1980s a core group of actuarial and financial professionals identified the immense risks to the defined-benefit model posed by ASOP and GASB standards and called for institutional reform (Himick and Brivot 2016, p. 34). The debate centered not only on the reform of specific standards, but on the standards-setting process and the intellectual foundations of the actuarial discipline itself, with a better integration with related disciplines (Gold 2016, p. 18)

The debate over "getting the accounting right" centers primarily on the proper way to discount plan liabilities, though it also broadly includes the need for a reconsideration of other methods that have the potential to obscure and shift plan costs into the future. While these flaws were known to some, a large analytical gap among actuarial, economic, and accounting methods in measuring pension liabilities and assets persisted due, in part, to moral hazard. Pension plan trustees and policymakers have an incentive to prefer overly optimistic estimates, rather than realistic estimates. This allows them to understate the true costs of pensions to taxpayers, freeing up budgetary dollars for more politically beneficial priorities.

The mirage, however, has become so far-fetched that many groups are starting to adopt their own actuarial assumptions to track the extent of unfunded pension liabilities. Moody's, for instance, replaced GASB reporting with its own evaluation to be more accurately reflect liabilities (Moody's 2013). Even the Bureau of Economic Analysis (BEA) has started producing its own data on state-level pensions to improve consistency and comparability of state and local pension data (Lenze 2020). To estimate funding ratios for public sector plans, the BEA uses a discount rate assumption consistent with the approach used to value private sector pensions by the Pension Benefit Guaranty Corporation (PBGD) or the yield on high-grade corporate bonds (Durant, Lenze, and Reinsdorf 2014, pp. 178–179).

4.5 Recent Reforms: The Role of Information and Lobbying

The emergence of the initial standards and recent reform of those standards are the product of both learning and lobbying. The Financial Crisis served as the catalyst for the recent reforms. The market crash transformed an abstract debate among professionals on actuarial cost methods and government reporting standards into a real fiscal crisis for municipal governments. This drew the attention of credit ratings agencies, journalists, analysts, and the public, putting pressure on governments for greater transparency in pension accounting and reporting (Allen and Petacchi 2015, p. 3).[30]

The controversy over how to value and report pension liabilities and set contribution policy is in no small part due to the fiscal consequences of adopting an approach that would present governments with far larger (and in some cases insurmountable) funding gaps and unrecognized (under their current reporting) liabilities. The "malleable actuarial approach" may be used to avoid presenting "unpleasant financial disclosures," creating an incentive for plan sponsors to resist the reform of pension accounting standards (Gordon and Jarvis 2003, p. 25). States experiencing fiscal stress have an even stronger incentive to understate pension costs and to overestimate expected returns when running deficits (Naughton et al. 2015, pp. 222 & 239). The presence of strong unions can even influence pension assumptions. States with strong unions are more likely to select discount rates to improve the appearance of funding in public financials (Bonsall, Comprix, and Muller 2019, p. 1301).

In addition to the fiscal effects, changing standards to reflect market valuation undermines the viability of the defined-benefit model in the public sector, a retirement option valued by many public employees and favored by politicians as a means of providing future benefits rather than immediate wage increases. When private sector accounting standards required firms to report the market value of pension plans in their financial statement, recognition of their costs was one factor that led companies to stop offering defined-benefit plans and to switch to defined-contribution plans for their employees (Foltin et al. 2017, p. 62). Changing standards in the public sector, would, justifiably, call into question the reliability and accuracy of actuarial science and government accounting fundamentals (Gold 2016, p. 15)

In the last decade, both ASB and GASB initiated efforts to modify and improve actuarial approaches and accounting standards (Kessler et al. 2019, pp. xi–xii). Actuarial standards have moved slowly, but definitively, toward market valuation approaches as well as recommending that actuaries incorporate risk analyses into actuarial reports. Government accountants landed on a compromise approach to valuing plan liabilities that was intended to satisfy both critics and defenders of the original disclosures.

---

[30] It is relevant to note that lobbying in accounting standards is not unique to US pensions. The incentive to present strong financials and optimistic scenarios is present in private and public sector accounting globally (Klumpes 1994).

GASB initiated a public pension reform project in 2006 to review its pension guide lines (Flesher et al. 2019, p. 70). In 2012, GASB 25 (1994a) was replaced with GASB 67 (2012a), which adopted a compromise approach to the question of what discount rate to use when valuing pension liabilities by suggesting the use of a "blended rate." The blended rate allows for sponsors to use the expected return on plan assets to value the funded portion of the liability and the return on a high-quality, tax-exempt municipal bond to value any unfunded portion of the liability. The compromise rule, however, did not address the fundamental measurement issue. It also did not reduce the incentive to manipulate discount rates in order to underreport liabilities and contribution amounts (Weinberg and Norcross 2017).

GASB 67 (2012a) introduces additional measurement distortions. Novy-Marx (2013, p. 30) finds that GASB 67 (2012a) violates at least two axioms for coherent risk measures.[31] The "blended rate" approach implies that it is possible to improve plan funding by "burning money." That is, a plan is better funded if it holds only high-risk assets, in order to justify a higher expected rate of return, than if it reduces the plan's risk, and thus the anticipated return, by adding additional "dollars" in the form of safer, but lower returning, bonds to the same high-risk portfolio (Novy-Marx 2013, p. 27). GASB 67 (2012a) allows for the application of different discount rates to the same portfolio of asset and liabilities based on how the plan partitions assets and liabilities for administrative purposes, enabling sponsors to lower their reported liability simply by dividing workers into separate plans (Novy-Marx 2013, p. 28).

GASB 27 (1994b) was replaced by GASB 68 (2012b), which adopted the approach of the financial sector and required that governments report the unfunded liability in their financial statements. GASB 68 (2012b), however, preserved a form of asset smoothing known as the "deferred inflow of resources," which allows actuaries to gradually recognize investment gains and losses rather than report the market value of assets.

The overall effect of GASB 67 (2012a) and 68 (2012b) was to more completely reflect pension liabilities in government financial statements. In fiscal year 2015, the first year of implementation, the inclusion of $537 billion in unfunded pension liabilities in states' balance sheet led states' net position to decline by 29 percent (Weinberg and Norcross 2017, p. 4).

---

[31] The four "coherent" properties of risk are defined in Artzner et. al. (1999) as "translation invariance," "positive homogeneity," "monotonicity," and "sub-additively." Novy-Marx shows that GASB 67 (2012a) violates translation invariance by implying that adding a dollar's worth of T-bills to a portfolio may weaken plan funding. Sub-additivity is violated if the plan can show improved funding status by partitioning plans administratively and dividing up assets and liabilities among them.

The resulting compromise rule to apply a blended rate to discounting liabilities did not satisfy either group of constituents, but rather gave the appearance of moving toward a financial economic approach while preserving discretion in the selection of discount rates to value plan liabilities. The requirement to apply a blended rate may have also led states to increase annual contributions to pension plans, in particular for states anticipating a significant financial impact from the new standards and states facing negative political and economic consequences for higher reported pension liabilities (Anantharaman and Chuk 2020, pp. 34–35).

In establishing these new standards, GASB undertook a multiyear process that included soliciting feedback from experts, governments, financial statement users, and the public. Allen and Petacchi (2015, pp. 24–25) find that states with poorly funded pension plans, high levels of corruption, and/or strict fiscal constraints were more likely to lobby against accounting changes that would increase the size of their reported liabilities. Arguments made against market valuation during the comments period included considerations of the effect of market valuation on the viability of public sector pension plans and the negative fiscal impact on government finances (Himick et al. 2016, p. 34), suggesting these were primary roadblocks toward reform. Despite only having fifteen members, the long-standing work of this core group of reformers advocating for the inclusion of financial economics helped shape the agenda and debate over the proper way to discount liabilities (Himick and Brivot 2016, p. 1).

In 2013, the Society of Actuaries (SOA) convened a blue-ribbon panel to review its methods in light of the deteriorating condition of pension funding over the preceding fifteen years and growing policymaker and public attention on the fiscal condition of plans. In its report, the SOA recommends actuaries disclose methods and assumptions and include a risk-free measure of pension liabilities based on the current risk-free rate adjusted for a risk premia (SOA Blue Ribbon Panel 2014, p. 8). The panel also recommended limiting the amortization period to between fifteen and twenty years and the length of asset smoothing to five years. Additionally, the panel offered recommendations on governance and plan stewardship, including improving information disclosure and training for trustees.

In 2014, the ASB began work on a new standard for delivering information to plan sponsors about potential risks to plan funding. Effective November 2018, ASOP 51 (Actuarial Standards Board 2017) includes risk assessment practices to test the effects of core actuarial assumptions, including investment returns, interest rates, and demographics based on market and plan experience, funding, assets, liabilities, and contribution policies.

ASOP 51 also recommends that public plan valuations include stress tests and scenario analyses incorporating economic shocks to reflect the risk of a broader range of expected returns on plan assets. Sensitivity analyses are also suggested to measure the effect of departures from key actuarial assumptions, including the discount rate, inflation, and mortality rates. Additionally, ASOP 51 recommends analysis to test the effects of a change in contributions from the sponsor. This may include the calculation of a "termination liability" at risk-free rates. And lastly, ASOP 51 also recommends that stochastic analyses be employed to project the likelihood of future events on plan funding (Fornia et al. 2019, p. 8).

Following ASOP No. 51, the ASB proposed a modification to ASOP No. 4 in 2018, in order to bring the actuarial approach closer to the principles of financial economics. The standard suggests that actuaries calculate the Investment Risk Defeasement Measure (IRDM), or a market value of the liability, based on either US Treasury yields or highly rated fixed-income debt in addition to presenting the actuarial value of liabilities based on the expected return on assets. While the return on highly rated debt is not exactly matched to the value of pensions that are default-free, IRDM internalizes the logic of discounting public pension liabilities at a risk-free rate for disclosure in actuarial reporting.

The improvement of actuarial standards as reflected in recent ASOPs is the result of a decades-long and often contentious debate on the methods and assumptions developed and used by the actuarial profession in producing valuation reports of state and local pension plans. It should be noted that as these practices are adopted and applied in valuation reports by actuaries, there remains the risk that governments statutorily embed fiscally evasive rules (Norcross 2010), that is, less demanding or potentially distortionary assumptions, to avoid presenting an economic accounting of pension assets and liabilities. For example, New Jersey statute requires that the plan actuaries employ an asset smoothing method that recognizes only 20 percent of investment gains and losses over a five-year period. This method does not meet the requirements of ASOP No. 44 and is reported as producing consistently biased estimates by the plan's actuaries (Public Employees' Retirement System of New Jersey 2020 p. 48). The effect of recognizing only a fraction of investment gains and losses creates a potentially non-correcting bias in estimating the actuarial value of assets. As long as the actuarial value of assets does not exceed the market value of assets by 50 percent, the formula produces an actuarial value of assets that is always positive (Norcross and Hardgrave 2011, p. 16).[32] New Jersey's Public

---

[32] Norcross and Hardgrave (2011) find that the formula tends to favor overvaluation over long periods of time driving down required contributions and funding ratios. A Monte Carlo simulation under a variety of market settings shows a tendency toward overestimation of assets that

Employee Retirement System (PERS) reports a market value of assets of $7.4 billion and actuarial liabilities of $25.6 billion in its fiscal year 2019 actuarial report, leaving the plan funded at 29.1 percent. Applying the statutorily defined smoothing formula produces a higher actuarial value of assets of $8 billion, which raises the funding ratio to 31.2 percent (Public Employees' Retirement System of New Jersey 2020, p. 8).

The presentation of some plan funding ratios in New Jersey was further enhanced in 2017 with the passage of the Lottery Enterprise Contribution Act (New Jersey Legislature 2017, p. 98). The act establishes the New Jersey Lottery Enterprise as an asset of the pension system and directs lottery proceeds to fund three of New Jersey's seven pension plans over thirty years.[33] Dedicating lottery proceeds to supplement the state's pension contribution is not itself problematic from a budgeting perspective – states typically dedicate lottery revenues to programmatic spending. The act is meant to make up for years of officials shirking on the annual contribution, a driving factor in the plan's underfunded status. From an accounting perspective, however, the presentation of this new funding stream in the legislation and actuarial reports treats projected lottery proceeds as certain.[34] The lottery was valued at $13.5 billion in the legislation and projected to bring in $37 billion in revenues over thirty years.[35] This special asset is presented as improving the plan's funding. The legislation allows actuaries to add a "special asset adjustment" to the actuarial value of assets in computing the funding ratio. In the case of the Public Employees Retirement System (PERS), the legislation dedicates 21.02 percent of the Lottery Enterprise's present value in that year to the plan's assets, which for the PERS plan amounts to $2.6 billion in fiscal year 2019. That amount is added to the actuarial value of assets, producing a higher asset value of $10.6 billion and, what the legislation calls a "target funded ratio," for the PERS plan of 41.6 percent (Public Employees' Retirement System of New Jersey 2020, pp. 3 & 8). Effectively, the actuarial report gives three different funding ratios depending on which asset value is used. The legislation further

---

does not self-correct until actuarial assets are overvalued by 50 percent relative to the market value of assets.

[33] The three largest funds in New Jersey are the Public Employees' Retirement System (PERS), The Teachers' Pension Annuity Fund (TPAF), and the Police and Firemen's Retirement System (PFRS), which, according to the statute, will receive 21.02, 77.78, and 1.02 percent of annual lottery proceeds, respectively.

[34] From a budgeting perspective, redirecting lottery revenues from funding existing state programs to fund the pension system presents the possibility of spending cuts or increased taxes to offset the loss of revenue to these programs.

[35] The Bank of America Merrill Lynch division was engaged by the state of New Jersey to produce the valuation of the Lottery Enterprise and earned $34 million in consulting fees. See Reitmeyer (2018).

specified what the "special asset adjustment" (or lottery pension revenues) should be for each year between fiscal years 2018 to 2022. For 2020, the legislation defines this amount as $1,070,451,102. However, due to the impact of COVID on the economy, lottery revenues declined by 11.6 percent in 2020, bringing in only $937 million. Due to the decline in lottery proceeds, the state reduced its annual contribution to the pension plans from $4.9 billion to $4.7 billion (Pensions & Investments 2020).

4.6 Conclusion

Actuarial methods and government accounting standards are central to understanding how defined-benefit pensions became a source of fiscal stress for many governments after the financial crisis of 2008. The conceptual and theoretical gaps among the actuarial profession, accounting standards-setting bodies, financial professionals, and economists concerning how to value, account for, and manage defined-benefit pensions has contributed to decades of misguided decision-making. It also led trustees to take on increasing levels of investment risk, while governments systematically underfunded accruing liabilities – even when contributing the actuarially recommended amount.

Reconciling the precepts of financial economics with the actuarial approach is an ongoing interdisciplinary project that has resulted in some improvements to actuarial standards. This decades-long effort highlights the impact that a core group of experts can have on influencing the epistemic approach of an entire discipline – an impact that was propelled by the Financial Crisis. Recent changes to actuarial standards include the incorporation of risk measures and analysis and the market valuation of assets and liabilities to plan valuations. GASB standards have progressed even more slowly. They now provide greater transparency in financial reports but do not fully embrace market valuation, which may produce new measurement distortions. Even as actuarial standards evolve and improve, the risk remains that plan trustees, policymakers, and governments embed fiscally evasive assumptions and methods into legislation in order to avoid confronting the full costs of funding the benefits promised to public sector workers.

5 Restoring Fiscal Accountability

Restoring fiscal accountability when it comes to state and local pensions in the United States requires addressing the previously described knowledge, incentive, and governance problems inherent to the current institutional structure of public pensions. In this Section, we offer a range of institutional solutions that would help alleviate each of these problems. We split our reforms into accounting reforms, governance reforms, and structural reforms. First, we discuss some of the most recent reforms.

Many of these reforms have already been successfully implemented in the private sector or have been adopted by some public pensions in the United States, although we strengthened our suggested reforms in some cases when we identified weaknesses with existing rules. This is particularly the case with pension rules for the private sector. While extending the currently existing rules applied to private sector pensions to the public sector would be a major improvement over the status quo, even the private sector's reforms have been insufficient (Bartram 2018; Coronado et al. 2008; Grant, Grant, and Ortega 2007).

5.1 Recent Reforms

Pension reforms are generally offered to either reduce accumulating costs on the sponsor or to improve plan funding in existing plans. In the period between 1999 and 2012, the majority of reforms focused on tweaking governance, such as changes to investment rules or to curtail political influence on decision-making (Thom 2017, p. 435). Other reforms included cost of living adjustment (COLA) reductions, raising the retirement age, and increasing vesting periods.

These reforms tended to be spurred by a "follow-the-leader" approach of copying reforms in other states rather than due to fiscal stress (Thom 2017, p. 438). Short-term fiscal stress, instead, often prompts legislators to increase employee contributions and adopt a "denial and delay strategy," where they opportunistically change their actuarial assumptions to misrepresent the severity of the funding crisis (Chen 2018, pp. 265 & 268).

Aubry and Crawford (2017) examine the post–Financial Crisis period of pension reform that focused tightly on reducing benefit generosity, particularly for new hires. Due to the legal protections surrounding pensions, benefit formulas for current employees are rarely altered. Between 2009 and 2014, 74 percent of state pension plans reduced benefit formulas. Only 26 percent of all state plans, however, altered benefits for existing employees. For local government pension plans, 57 percent of plans reduced benefits, but only 23 percent of all plans reduced benefits for current employees. The most common changes were increasing the retirement age, lengthening the vesting period, and reducing the benefit formula (Aubry and Crawford 2017, pp. 2 & 3). Reforms affecting current employees typically reduced COLAs or increased employee contributions (Aubry and Crawford 2017, p. 3).

When reforms are implemented, they are generally put in place only for newly hired employees, though current employees are often given the option to voluntarily move to the new plan. Opening up a reformed plan for new employees, however, was the least common reform (Aubry and Crawford 2017, p. 3). Since 2009, only eight states opened hybrid defined-benefit and defined-contribution plans for new hires or existing employees: Arizona, Connecticut, Michigan, Pennsylvania, Rhode Island, Tennessee, Utah, and Virginia (Bradford 2019). Four states opened plans for just new hires: Kansas and Kentucky created cash-balance plans, Oklahoma opened a defined-contribution plan for new state employees in 2015, and Michigan extended its defined-contribution plan for state employees to cover newly hired teachers in 2017.

Overall, defined-benefit plans remain the dominant model in the public sector, although some states offer employees an optional defined-contribution plan to supplement their defined-benefit plan. Several states, for instance, allow some occupational groups to select defined contribution as their primary plan, including Colorado, Florida, Indiana, Montana, North Dakota, Ohio, and South Carolina.[36] Universities in particular, often offer additional options more suited to their mobile faculty. A defined-contribution plan is the sole option offered to state university faculty in thirteen states (NASRA 2018). Eight states offer a defined-benefit plan to university faculty, while the remainder provide faculty the option to select either a defined-benefit or a defined-contribution plan (NASRA 2018). In competition for faculty who are often not served well by traditional public pension plans, universities, such as the University of Alabama and Auburn University, also offer additional defined-contribution retirement options on top of the traditional plan, meaning the sponsor is contributing to two retirement plans for each employee simply to offer a competitive retirement package to faculty who often do not stay at the same university throughout their career.[37]

Before the financial crisis of 2007–08 only three states – Michigan, Alaska, and West Virginia – moved new employees in some occupational groups to defined-contribution plans.[38] In 1997, Michigan was an early adopter of pension reform. Then-Governor Engler cited the state's history of erratic contributions, long vesting periods for employees, and projections that pointed to the possibility of it turning into a pay-as-you-go plan within twenty-five years. This became the basis for a "soft freeze" of the Michigan State Employees

---

[36] www.nasra.org/dc_plans#:~:text=A%20defined%20contribution%20plan%20is,to%20the% 20employee's%20retirement%20account.

[37] See https://hr.ua.edu/benefits/retirem and www.auburn.edu/administration/human_resources/ benefits/voluntary.html.

[38] The District of Columbia closed its defined-benefit plan and opened a defined-contribution plan in 1987.

Retirement System in which new hires were enrolled in defined-contribution plans (Dreyfuss 2011; Gilroy 2014). Current employees were given the option to switch to the new defined-contribution plan or to stay in the closed defined-benefit plan. Due to opposition from unions, the reform was not extended to teachers until 2017 (Oosting 2017). Alaska closed its teachers' and state employees' defined-benefit plans to new hires in 2006 (Nava 2014).

Even if reforms are enacted, they can be reversed under future political pressure. For instance, West Virginia closed its teachers' defined-benefit plan to new hires in 1991 but then re-opened it in 2005 under political pressure (Brull 2009).[39] The union voted to close the defined-contribution plan and migrate members' savings to the re-opened defined-benefit plan (Brull 2009). Alabama implemented a new plan with reduced benefits for new employees in 2012 (Dove and Smith 2016, p. 24) but has already rolled back some of these changes and, at least prior to COVID-19, was facing additional pressure from public employees to roll back even more changes (Scott 2019a & 2019b). Similarly, incentives to skip on contributions remain even after a plan is closed. Legislators in Michigan, for instance, under-contributed to the closed public employees' plan between 2002 and 2012, worsening its funding ratio (Hohman 2018). Similarly, Alaska legislators made inadequate contributions to their closed plan and continued to assume high returns on plan investments contributing to fiscal illusion and systematic underfunding (Nava 2014).

5.2 Accounting Reforms

As outlined, the complexities of pension accounting are exacerbated by the lack of transparency and the use of opportunistic accounting. While there is no surefire way to ensure that plan stakeholders actively monitor pension finances and hold sponsors and trustees accountable, increased professional, scholarly, and media attention on pension financial reporting and the fiscal implications of underfunded pension plans has led to some improvements in accounting and actuarial methods. Even more is needed.

The information contained in government financials and actuarial valuations should be made more easily accessible and intelligible to the public, more useful to decision makers, and more analytically transparent to experts. Where the economic basis for actuarial and accounting standards is absent and there is a high degree of discretion in the application of those standards, the result is

---

[39] The defined-contribution plan may have been ineptly implemented. Teachers claimed they received poor and limited advice on opening a defined-contribution plan with most individuals only meeting with sales representatives from one life insurance company. Nearly all those who switched to the defined-contribution option elected an annuity, despite other options being available from mutual funds and money market companies (Brull 2009).

public pension data that lacks reliability and comparability. This long-standing deficit in the accuracy of public pension reporting spawned an alternative academic and policy literature that uses economic and financial modeling tools to approximate pension liabilities and assets and assess investment risks.

The biggest opportunity for reform is in the area of establishing economically sound actuarial and accounting standards that support consistent and objective actuarial and accounting analysis of plan costs and performance rooted in financial economics. Simple reforms can be implemented to make understanding and evaluating public pension costs more accessible. These reforms address reporting, transparency, and risk assessment.

Pension reporting, making promises to current public employees, should be conservative in nature, to best ensure that such retirement promises are properly funded. Two of the most influential assumptions in actuarial reporting are the assumed rate of return for measuring the growth of assets and the assumed discount rate for discounting future liabilities. Both enable opportunistic accounting.

As mentioned earlier, public pensions often overstate the returns that can be realistically expected, meaning asset growth is overstated. This in turn, drives public pensions to invest in riskier asset classes to achieve their assumed rates of return. To put it another way, to maintain a fairly constant assumed rate of return in a declining-rate environment, public pensions are necessarily assuming a higher risk premium. There are three reasons that historical long-term rates of return should not be the primary guidepost for projecting assumed rates of return.

First, is the drop in real interest rates to unprecedented levels, most likely due to demographic factors (Rachel and Smith 2017) and, relatedly, a higher propensity to save (Hall 2017), especially in safer assets (Bean et al. 2015).[40] As can be seen in Figure 2, this means safe assets, including US government treasuries, are delivering much lower returns today than anytime in the recent past. While achieving 8 percent rates of return for a pension portfolio was a safe assumption when safe assets were delivering higher returns, it is a more unrealistic assumption in our current interest rate environment.

The second reason that historical returns should not be used as the primary determinant for projecting rates of return is that markets are volatile and can become under- or overvalued (Gjerstad and Smith 2014). For instance, the current price-to-earnings ratio of the S&P 500 is 38.[41] Compared to

---

[40] The factors driving the fall in interest rates is very much an open area of research. See Mankiw (2020).

[41] As of January 12, 2021, using trailing twelve-month earnings as reported. See www.multpl.com /s-p-500-pe-ratio.

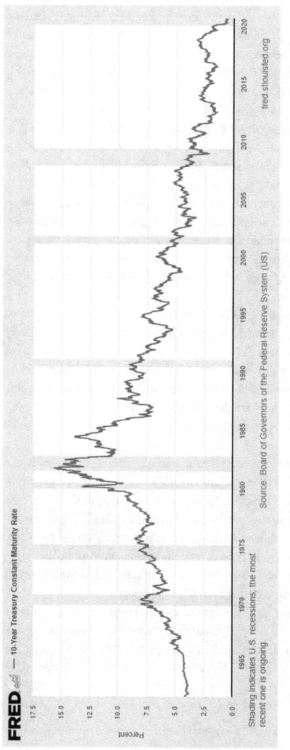

Figure 2 Ten-year treasury constant maturity rate

Source: Board of Governors of the Federal Reserve System (2021)

a historical average of between 14 and 16 (Shen 2000; Shiller 2015), this indicates that the market may be overvalued compared to the past. Historically, high price-to-earning episodes have been followed by periods of lower stock market returns (Asness 2012; Shen 2000; Trevino and Robertson 2002).

The third reason that historical returns should not be the guidepost for projecting future returns is that, out of fiduciary responsibility and concern for taxpayers, assumptions in public pension accounting should err on the side of being conservative. Downturns and recessions, while impossible to predict, can be expected to regularly occur. And, the impact of pension underfunding on local finances and government services, which only magnifies the effect of the economic downturn, are dire enough outcomes that they warrant conservatism.

Certainly, the toll of the Financial Crisis and COVID-19 on pension financial health provide recent examples of the dangers of overly optimistic assumptions. As Waring (2012, p. 41; emphasis in original) stresses, "Long term investors don't "get" the *expected* return; they receive a highly random and uncertain draw from an increasingly wide distribution of possible realized returns."

Despite the decline of real interest rates, the high price-to-earnings ratio, and the realized possibility of downturns, public pensions have not drastically revised their rate of return assumptions. The average rate among state public pensions has only declined to an average of 7.2 percent in Fiscal Year 2020 (NASRA 2020) with the lowest being 6.25 percent (Kentucky County) and the highest being 8 percent (Arkansas State Highway ERS and the Texas County & District).[42] This implies that their assumed risk premium (the assumed return above the risk-free rate) on average is 6 percent, well above the historical range of 3 to 4 percent (Biggs and Norcross 2020, p. 4).[43]

Reforming the use of optimistic assumed rates of return, however, represent a knowledge problem. While there is a consensus that current assumed rates of return for public pensions are too high (Stalebrink 2014; Vermeer, Styles, and Patton 2010), there is certainly dispute regarding what the correct rate should be. Complicating a concrete establishment of a rule for determining the assumed rate of return is the fact that portfolio allocations do vary between public pensions. Calculating returns for private placement investments, and other types of alternative investments, in particular, introduces wiggle room into the calculation.

---

[42] www.nasra.org//Files/medianandavgtimeseries.png and www.nasra.org/latestreturnassumptions.
[43] The notional fifteen-year Treasury yield rate was 1.2 percent in December 2020. See www.treasury.gov/resource-center/data-chart-center/interest-rates/Pages/TextView.aspx?data=yield

There are reforms, however, that can be implemented to mitigate this problem. The private sector, for instance, generally requires the use of a corporate bond yield to discount pension liabilities. Private pensions, however, were able to secure temporary relief (phasing out in 2021, if not extended) from discounting at the low rates that emerged in 2006 with the Pension Protection Act of 2006 (Anzalone and Clark 2019).[44]

One of the primary reasons that public pensions assume a high rate of return is because they are allowed by GASB accounting standards to utilize that assumed rate of return as the rate for discounting pension liabilities (Novy-Marx and Rauh 2009). However, the discount rate and the expected investment rate of return are independent in value. The expected rate of return on plan investments is simply that – an expectation of future returns on a given portfolio. As Waring notes, the discount rate to value a stream of future cash flows is not assumed, required, or expected but rather observed in the market in order to match the cash flows being discounted – in this case pension liabilities – with their market-equivalent in risk and timing of payment (Waring 2012, p. 28).[45] Public pension liabilities are bond-like. They are generally guaranteed-to-be-paid by governments and thus should be discounted at a risk-free rate. Selecting the discount rate to value pension liabilities should reflect the principles and practice of finance that includes the law of one price: any given cash flow has one price and therefore one set of discount rates.

> **Accounting Reform 1:** Prohibit the practice of using an assumed rate of return to discount pension liabilities. Pension assets and liabilities are independent in value and have substantially different risk profiles. The discount rate is observed in the market at any given point in time. Expected returns on the asset portfolio are not guaranteed but assumed, and thus should not be used for the purposes of discounting, regardless of the composition of the portfolio.

A related second reform would be to ensure that a risk-free rate of return be used to discount plan liabilities. Only a risk-free rate of return would reflect the guaranteed status of these liabilities. Any discount rate above the risk-free would imply that they were factoring into their actuarial assumptions the assumption that there were some possible scenarios where these liabilities would not be guaranteed. An appropriate risk-free rate of return would be either

---

[44] Some industries, such as airlines, government contractors, and charitable organizations were able to lobby to secure additional special rules and exemptions (Pension Protection Act of 2006; The Wall Street Journal 2007).

[45] As Waring (2012, p. 28) notes, technically one discount rate is not selected, but rather "the full curve of spot discount rates with each future cash flow discounted by the spot discount rate for its own time horizon."

the ten- or fifteen-year treasury (or an average of the two), whichever best fit the average length of the plan's liabilities.

> **Accounting Reform 2:** Require that a risk-free rate of return, such as the Ten-Year Treasury Bond rate, be used to discount liabilities to properly reflect their guaranteed status.

The process for determining the assumed rate of return should also be specified to ensure that the assumed rate of return on plan assets reflects a conservative estimate of the expected growth of plan assets over time. Simply using past historical returns, while certainly a metric that should be included in this calculation, is not sufficient. Reporting should reflect attempts to best reflect the consensus projection of stock and bond performance going forward, given long-term trends.

> **Accounting** Create a rule for determining the discount rate utilizing a reputable, and conservative, external prediction for equities and bonds, weighted by the pension's portfolio balance. Report funded health under a range of estimates to reflect the inherent risk incurred in the portfolio.

An often-overlooked assumption in public finance is the inflation rate. There is some evidence to suggest that inflation assumptions are opportunistically adjusted by public pensions (Biggs 2018).[46] A lower assumed rate of inflation implies a lower assumed rate of return, which would, by itself, be a conservative assumption (Peng 2009, p. 59). But, inflation assumptions have countervailing effects in actuarial calculations. If a public pension has a cost of living adjustment, then a lower inflation rate decreases these future liabilities. Also, actuarial assumptions typically include an assumed wage increase due to expected inflation. This has an effect on measures of pension health because final wages are a key metric in pension benefit formulas, so lowering the rate of expected inflation expectation will also decrease expected liabilities.

The current average assumed rate of inflation among public pension plans is 2.68 percent.[47] But compare this to the ten-year breakeven inflation rate of 1.69 percent[48] or even the new commitment by the Fed to embrace average inflation targeting of 2 percent.

---

[46] In fact, some public pensions, such as the Retirement Systems of Alabama, use different inflation assumptions for different calculations in their Comprehensive Annual Financial Reports.

[47] www.nasra.org/files/Issue%20Briefs/NASRAInvReturnAssumptBrief.pdf.

[48] https://fred.stlouisfed.org/series/T10YIE.

Accounting Reform 4: Require the use of a consistent, and reputable, inflation expectation throughout actuarial calculations. For instance, the Congressional Budget Office's inflation forecast in its Economic Outlook or the Federal Reserve Bank of St. Louis' Ten-Year Breakeven Inflation Rate.

Stress testing public pensions, by examining the funding health and governmental budgetary impact of down-side deviations from assumed variables, can play an important role in informing decision makers and the public about the risks they were incurring (Farrell and Shoag 2016). Mennis, Banta, and Draine (2018), for instance, recommend that stress testing be a standard practice for public pensions. In the past several years, multiple states have adopted stress testing and other risk assessment analyses as a means of evaluating the investment, demographic, and economic risks to plans.[49] In 2018, the ASB issued ASOP 51 enhancing actuarial risk assessments for public pensions to include modeling scenarios that threaten plan funding health. However, these methods continue to permit for actuarial discretion in conducting stress tests (Follett, Harrison, and Petrini 2021, p. 1)

Accounting Reform 5: Require stress testing and sensitivity analysis of pension plans so that funding health is reported under a range of possible scenarios. Stress testing evaluates the effect of various economic and demographic scenarios on funding. Sensitivity analysis tests the effect of the most significant actuarial assumptions on plan funding. Sensitivity analyses should also mandate modeling the impact of adopting a risk-free discount rate to value plan liabilities if the use of a risk-free rate is not required.

Given the riskiness and lack of transparency, in addition to the incentives for political allocation, when it comes to private placements, accounting, and reporting for private placements, public pensions need to utilize standardized, reputable, and transparent methods of evaluating these investments. Rather than estimating returns by aggregation, which prevents monitoring of individual performance (and variability and risk assessment), the size and returns of individual private placement investments should be reported individually.

Accounting Reform 6: Require private placements (or alternative investments) to utilize standardized, reputable, and transparent methods of evaluation to be annually audited by an external agency. This includes individual reporting on all private investments.

---

[49] These states include California, Colorado, Connecticut, Hawaii, Indiana, Montana, New Jersey, Pennsylvania, Vermont, Virginia, and Washington.

Certain actuarial practices are intended to dampen the recognition of costs by stretching them out over time. Asset smoothing – the gradual recognition of investment gains and losses – produces an "actuarial value of assets." It is a synthetic number that camouflages the market value of assets. Depending on the formula used, asset smoothing may embed hard-to-correct distortions in the actuarial value of assets leading to insufficient contributions. Actuarial standards limit the methods used to minimize such distortions. Politicians, however, may override actuarial advice and embed fiscally evasive methods in statutes or ordinances. Amortization methods may also be altered in state statute to get around actuarial standards. Illinois sets in statute an amortization method for five of its pension plans that requires actuaries to compute the annual contribution as a level percent of payroll sufficient to reach 90 percent of funding by 2045, effectively deferring payment on the unfunded liability and lowering the bar to full funding.[50]

In the private sector, amortization periods are typically five years, but were extended to seven years under the Pension Protection Act of 2006.[51] FASB recommends asset smoothing of five years.

> **Accounting Reform 7:** Prohibit the statutory adoption of actuarial assumptions that are intended to artificially inflate asset values, lower liabilities, or continually defer the cost of full funding for the purposes of depressing annual funding requirements. This includes the use of asset smoothing formulas that create biased estimates and do not comply with actuarial standards as well as amortization methods that do not comply with accepted practice in GASB 67/68.

5.3 Governance Reforms

Given the susceptibility of private placement investments to political opportunism, as well as the inherent difficulty of transparently reporting on their performance, a governance reform beyond Accounting Reform 6 would be to prohibit private placement investments altogether. These types of investments, while they can promise high returns, are also inherently risky.

> **Governance Reform 1:** Prohibit public pensions from making private placement (or alternative) investments. These investments are susceptible to both political pressure and opportunistic accounting.

---

[50] State of Illinois, State Actuary's Report, "The Actuarial Assumptions and Valuations of the State-Funded Retirement Systems," December 2018, p. 13. www.auditor.illinois.gov/Audit-Reports/Performance-Special-Multi/State-Actuary-Reports/2018-State-Actuary-Rpt-Full.pdf.

[51] Airlines got a special exemption and can use a seventeen-year amortization period (The Wall Street Journal 2007).

If private placement investments are not forbidden, to prevent additional avenues for potential corruption, conflict of interest disclosures (between the pension CEO and investment team and appointed leadership positions in the private placement) should be required for all associated board and executive leadership appointments.

> **Governance Reform 2:** Conflict of interest disclosures should also be required for all associated board members and the pension executive and investment leadership. They should detail any potential conflicts of interest or preexisting relationships with executive leadership appointments for private placement investments.

In addition to prohibiting the riskiest asset – private placements – public pensions may also be restricted to operate within allowable ranges of portfolio weights. Setting a rule ahead of time on the desired range of portfolio allocation would prevent public pensions from increasing risk to attempt to hide underperformance or underlying structural problems.

> **Governance Reform 3:** Set an allowable range of portfolio weights for each asset classification.

Fiduciary reviews can also be required so that board of trustee members and executive teams receive annual training and reviews on their fiduciary responsibilities. These types of reviews can help spot potential breaches of fiduciary responsibility due to simple "neglect, inadvertence, or incompetence" (Aneson 2016) before they become major problems. Miller and Funston (2014), for instance, suggest that a fiduciary review can answer the following questions:

- Are we meeting our fiduciary responsibilities?
- How do recent changes affect our fiduciary duties?
- How well are we managing potential conflicts of interest?
- Are governance processes working as well as they can/should?
- Do we have the most appropriate policies and practices?
- How are we doing compared to leading practices?
- Where can we improve?
- How can we be more effective and efficient?
- What is best for our fund and beneficiaries, given our current stage of development?

> **Governance Reform 4:** Require annual fiduciary reviews, not only to prevent fraud and corruption, but also to prevent breaches due to neglect, inadvertence, or incompetence.

5.4 Structural Reforms

Structural reforms are the most extensive reforms, but offer the greatest promise for finding a permanent solution to the public pension crisis. Plans at the most risk for defaulting on their promises to public employees will likely have to pursue these deeper structural reforms to avoid band-aid solutions that will simply alleviate the problem for a brief period.[52] Plans with the best funding health, however, can consider structural reforms to ensure that their pension plans don't become a problem later on.

One of the most drastic structural changes is actually quite simple in terms of knowing how to make the transition. That is transitioning away from a defined-benefit model to a defined-contribution model. A defined-contribution model offers many advantages to stakeholders over a defined-benefit model. Primarily, it benefits the public employees in that their employee and employer retirement benefits get put into an individual retirement account. That means that their retirement compensation is no longer based on questionable promises (Garon 2015). It is delivered upfront in an account owned by the employee. This way, the problem of underfunding is avoided because "the state is required to pay its share of the pension contribution in a timely manner so it can be invested in the employees' DC [defined-contribution] accounts" (Giertz and Papke 2007, p. 314). To increase public employee pay or retirement benefits would thus both require a current increase in taxes or a current reduction of benefits, helping restore the fiscal bridge between taxes and revenues that enables taxpayers to better evaluate cost and benefit of extensions jointly (Buchanan 1949; Shughart and Smith 2020). It would also ensure that the taxpayers receiving the current benefits from public employees would also be the same taxpayers paying the full costs for those public employees, preventing the abuses that emerge when benefits can be enjoyed now while costs are pushed into the future (Al-Bawwab and Smith 2020).

Furthermore, an individual retirement account offers the additional benefit to public employees of being portable, as there is no vesting period if employees move between jobs or even states or sectors (public to private employment). This is certainly a major benefit for those in higher education or spouses of military service members who typically move between states frequently. In some public pension plans, the vesting period is as long as ten years, meaning that those employees leaving before the end of the vesting period forfeit all their earned employer-side contributions.[53] This is particularly detrimental to the

---

[52] Temporary reforms that often only push the problem into the future may include COLA freezes or slight benefit reductions.

[53] They can even forfeit returns on their employee contributions. The Retirement Systems of Alabama, for instance, uses a formula to determine the interest received on employee contributions at withdrawal. An employee departing before seventeen years receives only 2 percent

retirement health of workers when the average tenure for state government workers is only 5.6 years and 6.6 years for local government workers, according to the Bureau of Labor Statistics.[54] Public pension employees need retirement options that will serve all public employees, even if they don't become career civil servants.

The most straightforward manner to implement this reform would be to put all new public employees into a defined-contribution system and to offer existing employees the option to transfer to the new system as well. Individual retirement accounts can be set up for public employees with a range of possible venders competing against each other. These companies have been reliably providing retirement accounts in the private sector for decades. Some of them, like TIAA, even operate as nonprofits. The range of account options could be structured to ensure that public employees stayed within a reasonable range of acceptable risk, while still allowing the employees to adjust their level of risk and expected return to reflect their own circumstances and risk tolerance. A default plan with a low-cost index fund with a portfolio that automatically moves toward safer asset classifications, such as bonds, as the employee gets closer to retirement, can be used to protect retirement accounts from market volatility using proven and accepted financial practices.

One factor that must be taken into consideration in transitioning from a defined-benefit to a defined-contribution pension model is the argument that there are additional 'transition costs' to wind down an existing plan. This claim is made based on the fact that a closed plan must shift its investments into safer, lower-yielding assets, and remain more liquid in order to pay out benefits to aging participants, thus requiring higher annual contributions from the sponsor. Biggs (2016) shows that this argument flows from public plans' reliance on expected rates of return on assets to value plan liabilities. Thus, this gives the false impression that the value of the liability can be lowered with a high-risk portfolio of investments. However, "the funding strategy adopted for a given liability does not change the value of the liability," itself (Biggs 2016, p. 5). A closed plan's liabilities are in fact decreasing since there are no new entrants. The shift to a lower-risk portfolio must be considered alongside the shrinking of total liabilities as the remaining participants age and retire.

---

interest on their contributions. See www.rsa-al.gov/uploads/files/TRS_Member_Handbook_2019.pdf.

[54] www.bls.gov/news.release/pdf/tenure.Pdf.

Structural Reform 1: Transition from a defined-benefit to a defined-contribution model providing employees with a transportable and secure retirement plan that can be invested to meet their own circumstances.

Absent the ability to enact the most promising structural reform (Structural Reform 1), the following structural reforms can help a defined-benefit public pension plan improve or preserve its funded health (National Conference on Public Employee Retirement Systems 2019). Some public pension plans, such as Maine and Wisconsin, have adopted automatic triggers. Based on prudent metrics for measuring public pension health utilizing actuarial science, these triggers kick in automatically when funded health dips below a designated threshold. For instance, triggers can automatically increase employee contribution rates or freeze benefit or COLAs until the pension plan's funded health reaches a designated optimum funded range, such as 100 to 110 percent. Private pensions, for instance, have a funding goal of 100 percent (EveryCRSReport.com 2020). Automatic triggers can also be utilized to ensure that healthy plans with excess funds, such as those with a funded ratio above 110 percent, be automatically used to reverse previous contribution rate increases, increase benefits to plan participants, or to decrease contribution rates. This provides some protection that a healthy public pension plan will not be "raided" for financing other state expenditures. These automatic triggers, however, depend on the aforementioned accounting reforms having been implemented to prevent plans from using opportunistic accounting to avoid the trigger by gaming the trigger metric.

Structural Reform 2: Establish automatic triggers that would increase contribution rates within an allowable range (1–3 percent) and freeze benefit rates and/or cost of living adjustments until the next review period. These automatic triggers should be tied to the funded ratio of the pension system and be operable until the pension plan hits a funded ratio target of 100–110 percent.

a. If the funded ratio exceeds the specified target, then excess funds should be used (1) to reverse previous contribution rates increases, (2) to increase benefits to plan participants, and (3) to decrease contribution rates.

A fairly straightforward way to curtail the growth of liabilities in pension plans with low funded health would be to eliminate guaranteed COLA adjustments. Importantly, ad hoc COLA increases should also be forbidden unless tied to an automatic trigger as mentioned in Structural Reform 2a.

Structural Reform 3: Eliminate guaranteed and ad hoc cost of living adjustments aside from those tied to an automatic trigger. Some of the worst-performing public pension plans are those that have allowed specific public employee groups, such as judges or state highway patrol officers, to lobby for special benefits unavailable to other groups of public employees. Such benefits may include lower employee contribution rates, higher employer contribution rates, or earlier retirement options. Requiring uniform benefits for public employees would ensure that groups could not lobby for these additional benefits, which compromise the health of the entire pension system.

Structural Reform 4: Make plan benefits uniform across groups of public employees. While tiered systems of varying rates among public employees should be allowed to facilitate reforms, all new public employees should receive the same contribution rates regardless of occupation to prevent public employee unions from securing additional benefits.

A final structural reform available for defined-benefit public pension plans would be to offer new employees a lower, guaranteed baseline benefit and a variable benefit linked to the funded ratio.

Structural Reform 5: Split postretirement benefits into a lower, guaranteed baseline benefit and a variable benefit linked to the funded ratio.

5.5 Conclusion

The fiscal risks presented by public sector pensions are the product of poorly designed rules that govern their valuation and stewardship. The defined-benefit plan – an annuity – if valued correctly and managed soundly should not present unknowable and catastrophic costs to the sponsor. Any set of pension reforms must consider two factors in order to be successful: the accuracy of financial and actuarial data and the incentives of policymakers to promise benefits while obscuring their costs. We offered three types of reforms to improve the institutions surrounding pension accounting, governance, and the structure of public sector retirement.

For many years, accounting and actuarial standards unintentionally provided cover for policymakers to avoid recognizing the full cost of funding benefits and opportunities to shift the financial burden in the future. The selection of discount rates, assumed rates of return, and inflation assumptions should be rules-based, rooted in economic theory, and reflect the practice of financial markets. There are not multiple subjective estimates of plan liabilities and assets. Assets and liabilities have objective values that should form the basis of determining the funding required to ensure that there are sufficient assets to meet obligations. Limiting the use of asset smoothing and amortization to dampen cost estimates and requiring stress testing and sensitivity analyses of plans will help to provide a clearer picture of plan funding and the resources required to meet obligations.

Improved actuarial and accounting standards still risk politicians avoiding them via state statute or local ordinance. Governance reforms should increase transparency in the management of plan assets and end the use of fiscally evasive actuarial methods and assumptions meant to suppress the true costs of plans. Investment policy, set by trustees, provides incentives to take risks with plan assets without providing full disclosure of their performance, and the opportunity for politicians to offer (undervalued) deferred compensation packages and negotiate with employee unions for more generous benefits while passing the risks on to taxpayers has limited the advancement of other retirement options for public employees.

Structural pension reform should consider how to increase options for public employees including the creation of defined-contribution plans. A defined-contribution plan binds the employer sponsor to make regular contributions to the employee's retirement account and puts the employee in control of their savings. Where defined-benefit plans remain in place, rules that bind politicians to make accurately calculated annual contributions to plans should be implemented.

As long as pension costs are partially recognized and opportunities to inflate asset values and minimize liabilities remain, plans remain at risk of serious underfunding. Identifying and eliminating incentives to underfund plans and undervalue benefits must be part of any successful pension reform. Accounting and actuarial rules have a major role in the performance of pensions but their slow reform is partly explained by the incentives facing politicians to promise benefits today and pass on the costs to the future. Decoupling public sector employees' retirement from the logic of politics is an essential step to fulfilling promises made to public employees.

6 Conclusion

The public pension funding crisis facing American state and local governments is a major threat to the viability of federalism. As state and local governments under duress cut traditional government services or hike taxes beyond what taxpayers are willing to bear, the likelihood of default on promises made to public sector workers or a federal bailout increase (Novy-Marx and Rauh 2014). Either would undermine the effectiveness and sustainability of federalist competition.

This would be a tragic loss, as well-functioning federalism is a founding principle of the United States. Competition between governments plays an essential role in preserving liberty and self-governance (Wagner 2015). A major reason for this is that voting with our feet between and within a federal system is one of the most important and effective forms of political expression and control we have (Somin 2020).

It is clear, however, that many state and local governments are gambling on a federal bailout especially when it comes to public pensions (Greve 2015, p. 40). Certainly, if federalism ever does collapse in the United States (likely in spirit rather than in name), public pensions will probably be the primary culprit.

While state and local bailouts previously seemed far-fetched, due to the understanding of the potentially devastating consequences of creating such a moral hazard problem in a federalist system, recent events have seemingly made these options more politically possible. City bankruptcies, such as Jefferson County and Detroit, and the bankruptcy of Puerto Rico, certainly demonstrated how strong the political pressure and popular sentiment for a bailout for problems caused in part by poorly managed pensions can be.

The downturn caused by COVID-19, similar to the Financial Crisis, put immediate pressure on the poor fiscal health of public pensions, exposing yet again the dangers of incentivizing risky portfolios. It is important to note that fiscally responsible states, who had better funded pensions, more responsible budgeting, and sufficient rainy-day funds have been better able to handle the downturn in economic activity caused by the pandemic. It is the states with preexisting problems, especially mounting unfunded pension liabilities, that were unprepared for a recession and thus suffered the most due to COVID. No one could be faulted for not predicting a global pandemic, but a major reason behind conservative fiscal prudence is knowing historically that we should expect periodic recessions, no matter their origins, and be prepared for them.

It should be no surprise that requests for federal aid to fund pensions were made by lawmakers in states known for systemically underfunding their plans over a period of decades. Illinois State Senate President Don Harmon asked the Illinois' Congressional Delegation to secure $10 billion in federal aid for pensions (Sidarova 2020). In May 2020, New Jersey Governor Phil Murphy similarly asked Congress to provide the state with $10 billion to close its budget gap. Absent a bailout, the Governor warned that 400,000 state workers would lose their jobs (Malanga 2020).

The unique circumstances of the pandemic unleashed a flurry of unprecedented programs, including lending facilities offered by the Federal Reserve, with a backstop from the US Treasury, to support state and local governments (Boettke et al. 2021, ch. 7; Cachanosky et al. 2020). Prior to this, the Federal Reserve had rejected interventions of this sort, specifically to avoid the associated moral hazard problems and political pressure that were sure to follow. Unsurprisingly, the Fed's lending facilities, initially available only to cities of more than one million and counties of more than two million, folded under political pressure and became available eventually to cities of 250,000 and counties of 500,000 residents (Politi and Smith 2020). As we finish this Element in December 2020, there is strong political pressure being exerted on the Federal Reserve to extend its lending facilities beyond the CARES Act designated closure date on December 31, specifically to enable more help to flow to state and local governments (*Wall Street Journal* 2020).

The emergence of public pensions as a major source of fiscal risk in US state and local governments is the result of the rules and political incentives surrounding their measurement and management. US state and local plans are subject to two forces: (1) the use of accounting assumptions and (2) actuarial techniques that dampen the full value of plan liabilities, inflate assets, encourage risk-taking in investments, or keep contribution levels tolerable for sponsors. These standards have been the subject of much criticism and discussion, prompting change within the actuarial profession and to its practices. Recent measurement reforms are laudable. They are also incomplete and slow-moving, in part due to the incentives facing some pension plan stakeholders to downplay or avoid the economic reality of the size of these unfunded obligations to public employees. Some of that avoidance on the part of politicians is pragmatic. Fully funding plans based on economic accounting would require significant budgetary trade-offs, particularly in the worst-funded states. Generations of political leaders have effectively abused the public trust and their fiduciary responsibility to public employees and taxpayers, preferring accounting maneuvers to economic reality and the fiscal discipline required to fully fund employee benefits.

The gravity of this situation stands in stark contrast to the disinterested "yawn" of voters. Despite its advantages, contemporary democracies are ill-equipped to handle problems of this nature (Brennan 2016). As discussed in this Element, the governance, accounting, and structure of public pensions exacerbate this problem, incentivizing inaction or even destructive behavior and misleading stakeholders. Reforms, as outlined in this Element, grounded in robust political economy, offer the only credible way to mitigate this problem. These reforms must be based on restoring the public's trust. Policymakers can either be complicit in the mirage or work today – against the intense pressure of entrenched interests – to put retirement benefits for public employees, and thus federalism itself, back on a sustainable course.

References

Actuarial Standards Board (2009). Actuarial Standards of Practice No. 44: Selection and Use of Asset Valuation Methods for Pension Valuations. www.actuarialstandardsboard.org/asops/selection-use-asset-valuation-methods-pension-valuations/.

Actuarial Standards Board (2013a). Actuarial Standards of Practice No. 1: Introductory Standards of Actuarial Practice. www.actuarialstandardsboard.org/asops/introductoryactuarialstandardpractice/.

Actuarial Standards Board (2013b). Actuarial Standards of Practice No. 4: Measuring Pension Obligations and Determining Pension Plan Costs and Contributions. www.actuarialstandardsboard.org/asops/measuring-pension-obligations-determining-pension-plan-costs-contributions/.

Actuarial Standards Board (2017). Actuarial Standards of Practice No. 51: Assessment and Disclosure of Risk Associated with Measuring Pension Obligations and Determining Public Pension Contributions. www.actuarialstandardsboard.org/asops/assessment-disclosure-risk-associated-measuring-pension-obligations-determining-pension-plan-contributions–3/.

Actuarial Standards Board (2020). Actuarial Standards of Practice No. 27: Selection of Economic Assumptions for Measuring Pension Obligations. www.actuarialstandardsboard.org/asops/selection-of-economic-assumptions-for-measuring-pension-obligations-effective-august-1-2021/.

Akerlof, George A. (1970). "The Market for "Lemons": Quality Uncertainty and the Market Mechanism," *The Quarterly Journal of Economics* 84(3): 488–500.

Al-Bawwab, Rania and Daniel J. Smith (2020). "Breaking Bad: Public Pensions and the Loss of that Old-Time Fiscal Religion," *The Independent Review: A Journal of Political Economy* 25(1).

Allen, Abigail and Reining Petacchi (2015). "Public Pension Accounting Reform: Preparer Incentives and User Interest," Harvard Business School Accounting & Management Unit Working Paper 15–043. www.hks.harvard.edu/centers/mrcbg/programs/growthpolicy/public-pension-accounting-reform-preparer-incentives-and-user.

American Academy of Actuaries (2012). "The 80% Pension Funding Standard Myth," Issue Brief (July). www.actuary.org/sites/default/files/files/80_Percent_Funding_IB_071912.pdf.

Anantharaman, Divya and Elizabeth Chuk (2020). "The Impact of Governmental Accounting Standards on Public Sector Pension Funding," SSRN Working Paper. https://papers.ssrn.com/sol3/papers.cfm?abstract_id=2533492.

Andonov, Aleksander (2014). "Pension Fund Asset Allocation Performance," a thesis submitted for the Degree of Doctor of Philosophy at Maastricht University, May 21, 2014.

Andonov, Aleksander, Rob M. M. J. Bauer, and K. J. Martin Kremers (2017). "Pension Fund Asset Allocation and Fund Discount Rates," *Review of Financial Studies* 30(9): 2555–2595.

Andonov, Aleksandar, Yael V. Hochberg, and Joshua D. Rauh (2018). "Political Representation and Governance: Evidence from Investment Decisions of Public Pension Funds," *The Journal of Finance* 73(5): 2041–2086.

Anenson, T. Leigh (2016). "Public Public Pensions and Fiduciary Law: A View From Equity," *University of Michigan Journal of Law Reform* 50: 251–290.

Anzalone, Joe and Michael Clark (2019). "The End of Interest Rate Relief is Coming," *Pension&Investments*. June 3rd. www.pionline.com/article/ 20190603/ONLINE/190609999/commentary-the-end-of-interest-rate-relief-is-coming.

Anzia, Sarah F. and Terry M. Moe (2015). "Public Sector Unions and the Costs of Government," *The Journal of Politics* 77(1): 144–127.

Anzia, Sarah F. and Terry M. Moe (2017). "Polarization and Policy: The Politics of Public- Sector Pensions," *Legislative Studies Quarterly* 42(1): 33–62.

Anzia, Sarah F. and Terry M. Moe (2019). "Interest Groups on the Inside: The Governance of Public Pension Funds," *Perspectives on Politics* 17(4): 1059–1078.

Artzner, Philippe, Freddy Delbaen, Jean-Marc Eber, and David Heath (1999). "Coherent Measures of Risk," *Mathematical Finance* 9(3): 203–228.

Asness, Clifford S. (2012). "An Old Friend: The Stock Market's Shiller P/E," AQR: Capital Management.

Aubry, Jean-Pierre, Anqi Chen, Patrick M. Hubbard, and Alicia H. Munnell (2020). "ESG Investing and Public Pensions: An Update," Center for Retirement Research at Boston College State and Local Pension Plans, No. 74 (October). https://crr.bc.edu/wp-content/uploads/2020/10/SLP74.pdf.

Aubry, Jean-Pierre and Caroline V. Crawford (2017). "State and Local Pension Reform Since The Financial Crisis," *Center for Retirement Research at Boston College*, 54: 1–10.

Bader, Lawrence N. and Jeremy Gold (2003). "Reinventing Pension Actuarial Science," *Pension Forum Book* 14(2): 1–39.

Bagchi, Sutirtha (2019). "The Effects of Political Competition on the Generosity of Public- Sector Pension Plans," *Journal of Economic Behavior and Organization* 164: 439–468.

Bahl, Roy W. and Bernard Jump (1974). "The Budgetary Implications of Rising Employee Retirements System Costs," *National Tax Journal* 27(3): 479–490.

Bartram, Söhnke M. (2018). "In Good Times and in Bad: Defined-Benefit Pensions and Corporate Financial Policy," *Journal of Corporate Finance* 48: 331–351.

Bean, Charles, Christian Broda, Takatoshi Ito, and Randall Kroszner (2015). "Low for Long? Causes and Consequences of Persistently Low Interest Rates," *Geneva Reports on the World Economy*, International Center for Monetary and Banking Studies 17.

Beermann, Jack M. (2013). "The Public Pension Crisis," *Washington and Lee Law Review* 7(1): 1–94.

Begenau, Juliane and Emil Siriwardane (2020). "How Do Private Equity Fees Vary Across Public Pensions?" Harvard Business School Working Paper, No. 20–073. www.hbs.edu/faculty/Pages/item.aspx?num=57534.

Biggs, Andrew (2016). "Are There Transition Costs to Closing a Public-Employee Retirement Plan?" Mercatus Research, Mercatus Center at George Mason University, Arlington, VA, August 2016.

Biggs, Andrew (2018). "Public Sector Pensions Assume Record-High Investment Returns," Forbes. December 4th. www.forbes.com/sites/andrew biggs/2018/12/04/public-sector-pensions-assume-record-high-investment-returns/#e3c88406ec5c.

Biggs, Andrew and Eileen Norcross (2020). "Public Sector Pensions and the COVID-19 Shock," Mercatus Center at George Mason University Policy Brief: Special Edition. www.mercatus.org/publications/covid-19-crisis-response/public-sector-pensions-and-covid-19-shock#:~:text=The%20COVID %2D19%20pandemic%20was,localities%20can%20ill%20afford%20it.

Bleakney, Thomas P. (1973). "Problems and Issues in Public Employee Retirement Systems," *The Journal of Risk and Insurance* 40(1): 39–46.

Board of Governors of the Federal Reserve System (US), 10-Year Treasury Constant Maturity Rate [GS10], retrieved from FRED, Federal Reserve Bank of St. Louis. https://fred.stlouisfed.org/series/GS10.

Boettke, Peter J., Christopher Coyne, Peter T. Lesson, and Frederic Sautet (2005). "The New Comparative Political Economy," *Review of Austrian Economics* 18(3/4): 281–304.

Boettke, Peter J. and Peter T. Leeson (2004). "Liberalism, Socialism, and Robust Political Economy," *Journal of Markets and Morality* 7(1): 99–111.

Boettke, Peter J., Alexander W. Salter, and Daniel J. Smith (2021). *Money and the Rule of Law*. Cambridge University Press.

Boettke, Peter J. and Daniel J. Smith (2010). "Private Solutions to Public Disasters: Self-Reliance and Social Resilience." In William Kern (ed.), *Private Solutions to PublicDisasters: Self-Reliance and Social Resilience*. Western Michigan University Press, pp.87–102.

Bosnall IV, Samuel B., Joseph Comprix, Karl A. Muller III (2019). "State Pension Accounting Estimates and Strong Public Unions," *Contemporary Accounting Research* 36(3): 1299–1336.

Boyd, Donald J. and Yimeng Yin (2016). "Public Pension Funding Practices," Pension Simulation Project, Rockefeller Institute of Government at State University of New York.

Bradford, Hazel (2019). "Public Plans Surf Wave of Reforms in Aftermath of Crisis." *Pensions & Investments*, February 18th. www.pionline.com/article/20190218/PRINT/190219876/public-plans-surf-wave-of-reforms-in-after math-of-crisis.

Bradley, Daniel, Christos Pantzalis, and Xiaojing Yuan (2016). "The Influence of Political Bias in State Pension Funds," *Journal of Financial Economics* 119(1): 69–91.

Brennan, Jason (2016). *Against Democracy*. Princeton University Press.

Brennan, Jason (2011). *The Ethics of Voting*. Princeton University Press.

Bronner, David (2015). "Johnson Center a Poor Steward of Facts Where RSA Concerned," AL.com. July 31st. www.al.com/opinion/2015/07/johnson_cen ter_a_poor_steward.html.

Brown, Jeffrey R. and George G. Pennacchi (2016). "Discounting Pension Liabilities: Funding vs. Value," *Journal of Pension and Economic Finance* 15(3): 254–284.

Brown, Jeffrey R., Joshua M. Pollett, and Scott J. Weisbenner (2015). "The In-State Equity Bias of State Pension Plans," NBER Working Paper No. 21020.

Brown, Jeffrey R. and David W. Wilcox (2009). "Discounting State and Local Pension Liabilities," *American Economic Review* 99(2): 538–42.

Brull, Stephen (2009). "Pension U Turn," *Institutional Investor*, February 12th. www.institutionalinvestor.com/article/b150q9p95qfpy1/pension-u-turn.

Buchanan, James M. (1949). "The Pure Theory of Government Finance: A Suggested Approach," *Journal of Political Economy* 56(6): 496–505.

Buchanan, James M. (1960[2001]). ""La Scienz Della Finanze": The Italian Tradition in Fiscal Theory." In *Externalities and Public Expenditure Theory*, Volume 15 of *The Collected Works of James M. Buchanan*. Liberty Fund Inc., pp. 59–105.

Buchanan, James M. and Richard E. Wagner (1977[2000]). *Democracy in Deficit*. Liberty Fund Inc.

Cachanosky, Nicolas, Bryan Cutsinger, Thomas L. Hogan, William J. Luther, and Alexander William Salter (2020). "The Federal Reserve's Response to the COVID-19 Contraction: An Initial Appraisal," AIER Sound Money Project Working Paper No. 2021–01. https://papers.ssrn.com/sol3/papers .cfm?abstract_id=3726345.

Canary, Leura G. (2015). Retirement Systems of Alabama Public Presentation to the Joint Committee on Alabama Public Pensions. October 5th. Montgomery, Alabama.

Caplan, Bryan (2007). *The Myth of the Rational Voter.* Princeton University Press.

Chan, Albert P. C. and Emmanuel Kingsford Owusu (2017). "Corruption Forms in the Construction Industry: Literature Review," *Journal of Construction Engineering and Management,* 143(8): 04017057.

Chen, Gang (2018). "Understanding the Decisions in State Pension Systems: A System Framework," *The American Review of Public Administration* 48 (3): 260–273.

Chaney, Barbara A., Paul A. Copley, and Mary S. Stone (2002). "The Effect of Fiscal Stress and Balanced Budget Requirements on the Funding and Measurement of State Pension Obligations," *Journal of Accounting and Public Policy* 21(4&5): 287–313.

Clark, Gordon L., Emiko Caerlewy-Smith and John C. Marshall (2006). "Pension Fund Trustee Competence: Decision Making in Problems Relevant to Investment Practice," *Journal of Pension Economics and Finance* 5(1): 91–110.

Clark, Gordon L. and Tessa Hebb (2004). "Pension Fund Corporate Engagement: The Fifth Stage of Capitalism," *Industrial Relations* 59(1): 142–171.

Coggburn, Jerrell D. and Richard C. Kearney (2010). "Trouble Keeping Promises? An Analysis of Underfunding in State Retiree Benefits," *Public Administration Review* 70(1): 97–108.

Coffee Jr., John C. (1991). "Liquidity versus Control: The Institutional Investor as Corporate Monitor," *Columbia Law Review* 91(6): 1277–1368.

Coggburn, Jerrell, D. and Christopher G. Reddick (2007). "Public Pension Management: Issues and Trends," *International Journal of Public Administration* 30(10): 995–1020.

Coronado, Julia L., Eric M. Engen, and Brian Knight (2003). "Public Funds and Private Capital Markets: The Investment Practices and Performance of State and Local Pension Funds," *National Tax Journal* LVI(3): 579–594.

Coronado, Julia L., Olivia S. Mitchell, Steven A. Sharpe, and S. Blake Nesbitt (2008). "Footnotes Aren't Enough: The Impact of Pension Accounting on Stock Values," *Journal of Pension Economics and Finance* 7(3): 257–276.

Costrell, Robert M. (2012a). "'GASB Won't Let Me' – A false Objection to Public Pension Reform," *Pensions & Investments.* Laura and John Arnold Foundation Policy Perspective. https://citeseerx.ist.psu.edu/viewdoc/download?doi=10.1.1.707.5183&rep=rep1&type=pdf.

Costrell, Robert M. (2012b). Memo to Mr. Thomas J. Cavanaugh and Dr. Brent A. Banister. June 20th. www.uaedreform.org/wp-content/uploads/2000/01/Costrell-reply-to-Cavanaugh-MacDonald.pdf.

Costrell, Robert M. (2018). "Cross-Subsidization of Teacher Pension Benefits: The Impact of the Discount Rate," *Journal of Pension Economics and Finance* 19(2): 147–1622.

Da Empoli, Domenico (2002). "The Theory of Fiscal Illusion in a Constitutional Perspective," *Public Finance Review* 30(5): 377–384.

DeAngelis, Corey A. (2018). "Police Choice: Feasible Policy Options for a Safer and Freer Society," *Libertarian Papers* 10(2): 179–206.

Dell'Anno, Roberto and Paulo Mourão (2012). "Fiscal Illusion Around the World: An Analysis Using the Structural Equation Approach," *Public Finance Review* 40(2): 1–30.

DiSalvo, Daniel (2018). *The Politics of Public Pension Boards*. Manhatten Institute.

Dobra, Matt and Bruce H. Lubich (2013). "Public Pension Governance and Asset Allocation," *JCC: The Business and Economics Research Journal* 6 (1): 83–101.

Dollery, Brian E. and Andrew C. Worthington (1996). "The Empirical Analysis of Fiscal Illusion," *Journal of Economic Surveys* 10(3): 261–297.

Dove, John A., Courtney A. Collins, and Daniel J. Smith (2018). "The Impact of Public Pension Board of Trustee Composition on State Bond Ratings," *Economics of Governance* 19: 51–73.

Dove, John A. and Daniel J. Smith (2016). "Alabama at the Cross-Roads." Mercatus Center at George Mason University. www.mercatus.org/system/files/Dove-Alabama-v3.pdf.

Downs, Anthony (1960). "Why the Government Budget Is Too Small in a Democracy," *World Politics*, July.

Dreyfuss, Richard C. (2011). "Estimated Savings from Michigan's 1997 State Employees Pension Plan Reform," Policy Brief, Mackinac Center for Public Policy. June 23rd. www.mackinac.org/archives/2011/2011-03PensionFINAL web.pdf.

Durant, Dominique, David Lenze, and Marshall B. Reinsdorf (2014). "Adding Actuarial Estimates of Defined-Benefit Pension Plans to National Accounts." In Charles R. Hulten and Marshall B. Reinsdorf (eds.), *Measuring Wealth and Financial Intermediation and Their Links to the Real Economy*. National Bureau of Economic Research, Inc., pp. 151–203.

Dyck, Alexander, Paulo Martins Manoel, and Adair Morse (2019). Working Paper. http://faculty.haas.berkeley.edu/morse/research/papers/DyckMorseManoel.pdf.

Easterday, Kathryn E. and Tim V. Eaton (2012). "Double (Accounting) Standards: A Comparison of Public and Private Sector Defined Benefit Pension Plans," *Journal of Public Budgeting, Accounting & Financial Management* 24(2): 278–312

Eaton, Tim V. and John R. Nofsinger (2004). "The Effects of Financial Constraints and Political Pressure on the Management of Public Pension Funds," *Journal of Accounting and Public Policy* 23(2): 161–189.

Epple, Dennis and Katherine Schipper (1981). "Municipal Pension Funding: A Theory and Some Evidence," *Public Choice* 37: 141–178.

Epstein, Gerald and Jessica Carrick-Hagenbarth (2011). "Avoiding Group Think and Conflicts of Interest: Widening the Circle of Central Bank Advice," *Central Banking Journal*.

Eusepi, Giuseppe and Richard E. Wagner (2017). *Public Debt: An Illusion of Democratic Political Economy*. Edward Elgar Publishing.

EveryCRSReport.com (2020). "Single-Employer Defined Benefit Pension Plans: Funding Relief and Modifications to Funding Rules." www.everycrsre port.com/reports/R46366.html#_Toc40885553.

Exley, C. J., S. J. B. Mehta, and A. D. Smith (1997). "The Financial Theory of Defined Benefit Pension Schemes," *British Actuarial Journal* 3(4): 835–966.

Fabo, Brian, Martina Jančoková, Elisabeth Kempf, and Ľuboš Pástor (2020). "Fifty Shades of QE: Conflicts of Interest in Economic Research," NBER Working Paper No. 27849.

Farrell, James and Daniel Shoag (2016). "Risky Choices: Stimulating Public Pension Funding Stress with Realistic Shocks," Harvard Kennedy School Working Paper Series RWP16-053. https://papers.ssrn.com/sol3/papers.cfm?abstract_id=2887672.

Financial Accounting Standards Board (FASB) 1980a. *Accounting and Reporting by Defined Benefit Plans*. SFAS No. 35. Norwalk, CT: FASB

Fink, Alexander and Richard E. Wagner (2013). "Political Entrepreneurship and the Formation of Special Districts," *European Journal of Law and Economics* 35: 427–439.

Fisk, Catherine L. and Song Richardson (2017). "Police Unions," *George Washington Law Review* 84: 712–799.

Flesher, Dale L., Craig Foltin, Gary John Previts, and Mary S. Stone (2019). "A Comprehensive Review of the Evolution of Accounting Standards for State and Local Government Pensions and Other Postemployment Benefits in the United States," *Accounting Historians Journal* 46(1): 57–77.

Follett, Tatiana, Noah Harrison, and Anna Petrini (2021). "Public Pension Stress Testing in the States," National Conference of State Legislatures.

https://www.ncsl.org/research/fiscal-policy/public-pension-stress-testing.aspx.

Foltin, Craig, Dale L. Flesher, Gary J. Previts, and Mary S. Stone (2017). "State and Local Government Pensions at the Crossroads: Updated Accounting Standards Highlight the Challenges," *The CPA Journal* 87(4): 42–51.

Forman, Jonathan Barry (2009). "Funding Public Pension Plans," *John Marshall Law Review* 42(4): 837–878.

Fornero, Elsa and Anna Lo Prete (2019). "Voting in the Aftermath of a Pension Reform: The Role of Financial Literacy," *Journal of Pension Economics & Finance* 18(1): 1–30.

Fornia, William, Paul Angelo, Randy Dziubek, and Todd Tauzer (2019). "Decision-Useful Risk Measures for Public Pensions," *In the Public Interest*, 19: 6–22.

Galbraith, John K. (1958). *The Affluent Society*. Houghton-Mifflin.

Garon, Jean-Denis. 2015. "The Commitment Value of Prefunded Pensions," CESifo Working Paper Series NO. 5658. http://papers.ssrn.com/sol3/papers.cfm?abstract_id=2719466.

Gjerstad, Steven D. and Vernon L. Smith (2014). *Rethinking Housing Bubbles*. Cambridge University Press.

Giertz, J. Fred and Leslie E. Papke (2007). "Public Pension Plans: Myths and Realities for State Budgets," *National Tax Journal* 60(2): 305–23.

Gilroy, Leonard (2014). "Pioneering State-Level Pension Reform in Michigan," Reason Foundation. February 21st. https://reason.org/commentary/pension-reform-michigan/.

Grant, C. Terry, Gerry H. Grant, and William R. Ortega (2007). "FASB's Quick Fix for Pension Accounting Is Only First Step," *Financial Analysts Journal* 63(2): 21–35.

Greve, Michael S. (2015). *Federalism and the Constitution*. Mercatus Center at George Mason University. www.mercatus.org/system/files/Greve-web-6-3-15.pdf.

Gribbin, D. J. (2019). "Why Is Federal Infrastructure Policy So Difficult?" Brookings Institute, *The Avenue*. February 28th. www.brookings.edu/blog/the-avenue/2019/02/28/why-is-federal-infrastructure-policy-so-difficult/.

Gold, Jeremy (2003). "Risk Transfer in Public Pensions." In Olivia S. Mitchell and Kent Smetters (eds.), *The Pension Challenge: Risk Transfers and Retirement Income Security*. Oxford University Press, pp. 102–115.

Gold, Jeremy (2016). "Public Pension Crisis: Role of the Actuarial Profession," *In the Public Interest* 12: 15–19.

Gorina, Evgenia (2018). "City Revenue Structure and Unfunded Pension Liabilities," *State and Local Government Review* 50(3): 189–202.

Gordon, Tim and Stuart Jarvis (2003). "Financial Economics and Pension Actuaries: The UK Experience," presented at "The Great Controversy: Current Pension Actuarial Practice In Light of Financial Economics Symposium," Vancouver, Society of Actuaries. www.soa.org/globalassets/assets/Library/Monographs/Retirement-Systems/The-Great-Controversy/2004/June/m-rs04-1-17.pdf.

Governmental Accounting Standards Board (1994a). Statement No. 25: Financial Report for Defined Benefit Pension Plans and Notes and Note Disclosures for Defined Contribution Plans. www.gasb.org/jsp/GASB/Document_C/DocumentPage?cid=1176160029908&acceptedDisclaimer=true.

Governmental Accounting Standards Board (1994b). Statement No. 27: Accounting for Pensions by State and Local Government Employers. www.gasb.org/jsp/GASB/Document_C/DocumentPage?cid=1176160029312&acceptedDisclaimer=true.

Governmental Accounting Standards Board (2012a). Statement No. 67: Financial Reporting for Pension Plans. www.gasb.org/jsp/GASB/Document_C/DocumentPage?cid=1176160220594&acceptedDisclaimer=true.

Governmental Accounting Standards Board (2012b). Statement No. 68: Accounting and Financial Reporting For Pension Plans. www.gasb.org/jsp/GASB/Document_C/DocumentPage?cid=1176160220621&acceptedDisclaimer=true.

Hall, Adren and Hal Hovey (1980). "State and Local Government Retirement Systems: Problems and Prospects," *National Tax Journal* 33(3): 371–380.

Hall, Robert E. (2017). "Low Interest Rates: Causes and Consequences," *International Journal of Central Banking* 50 (September): 103–117.

Hess, David (2005). "Protecting and Politicizing Public Pension Fund Assets: Empirical Evidence on the Effects of Governance Structures and Practices," *University of California Davis Law Review* 39: 187–224.

Hess, David and Gregorio Impavido (2004). "Governance of Public Pension Funds: Lessons from Corporate Governance and International Evidence." In Alberto R. Musalem and Robert J. Palacios (eds.), *Public Pension Fund Management*, World Bank, pp. 49–89.

Hess, Frederick M. and Juliet P. Squire (2010). ""But the Pension Fund Was Just SITTING There . . . ": The Politics of Teacher Retirement Plans," *Education Finance and Policy* 5(4): 587–616.

Higgs, Robert (1987). *Crisis and Leviathan*. Oxford University Press.

Himick, Darlene and Mario Brivot (2018). "Carries of Ideas in Accounting Standard-Setting and Financialization: The Role of Epistemic Communities," *Accounting, Organizations and Society* 66(c): 29–44.

Himick, Darlene, Marion Brivot and Jean-Francois Henri (2016). "An Ethical Perspective On Accounting Standards Setting: *Professional and Lay-Experts Contribution to GASB's Pension Project,"* *Critical Perspectives in Accounting* 36: 22–38.

Hochberg, Yael V. and Joshua D. Rauh (2013). "Local Overweighting and Underperformance: Evidence from Limited Partner Private Equity Investments," *Review of Financial Studies* 26(2): 403–451.

Hoepner, Andreas and Lisa Schopohl (2019). "State Pension Funds and Corporate Social Responsibility: Do Beneficiaries' Political Values Influence Funds' Investment Decisions?" *Journal of Business Ethics* 165: 489–516.

Hohman, James (2018). "Michigan Catching up on its State Employee Pension Debt," Mackinac Center blog, August 1st. www.mackinac.org/michigan-catching-up-on-state-employee-pension-debt.

Holcombe, Randall G. (2002). "Political Entrepreneurship and the Democratic Allocation of Economic Resources," *The Review of Austrian Economics* 15: 143–159.

IGM Forum (2012). "U.S. State Budgets." *Chicago Booth.* www.igmchicago .org/surveys/u-sstate-budgets.

Illinois State Actuary Report (2018), "The Actuarial Assumptions and Valuations of the State-Funded Retirement Systems," December 2018. www.auditor.illinois.gov/Audit-Reports/Performance-Special-Multi/State-Actuary-Reports/2018-State-Actuary-Rpt-Full.pdf.

Inman, Robert P. (1981). "'Municipal Pension Funding: A Theory and Some Evidence' by Dennis Epple and Katerine Schipper: A Comment," *Public Choice* 37(1): 179–187.

Inman, Robert P. (1982). "Public Employee Pensions and the Local Labor Budget," *Journal of Public Economics* 19: 49–71.

Ivashina, Victoria and Josh Lerner (2018). "Looking for Alternatives: Pension Investments around the World, 2008 to 2017," Working Paper. www.hks .harvard.edu/centers/mrcbg/programs/growthpolicy/looking-alternatives-pension-investments-around-world–2008–2017.

Johnson, Richard W. (1997). "Pension Underfunding and Liberal Retirement Benefits Among State and Local Government Workers," *National Tax Journal* 50(1): 113–42.

Kaspar, Daniel J. (2011). "Defined Benefits, Undefined Costs: Moving Towards a More Transparent Accounting of State Public Employee Pension Plans," *William & Mary Policy Review* 3(1): 129–156.

Kessler, Emily, Robert Stein, Gregory Mennis, Susan Banta, Thomas J. Healy, and Fatima Yousofi (2019). "Better Measurements: Risk Reporting for Public Pension Plans*" M-RCBG Associate Working Paper Series No. 28,*

Mossavar-Rahmani Center for Business and Government, Harvard Kennedy School, Cambridge, MA.

Kiewiet, D. Roderick and Mathew D. McCubbins (2014). "State and Local Government Finance: The New Fiscal Ice Age," *Annual Review of Political Science* 17: 105–122.

Klumpes, P. J. M. (1994). "The Politics of Rule Development: A Case Study of Australian Pension Fund Accounting Rule-Making," *Abacus* 30(2): 140–159.

Kotlikoff, Laurence J. and Scott Burns (2012). *The Clash of Generations: Saving Ourselves, Our Kids, and Our Economy*. The MIT Press.

Lawson, Brian (2012). "Alabama House Speaker Wants Changes to State Retirement Systems," AL.com. January 15th. www.al.com/breaking/2012/01/alabama_house_speaker_wants_ch.html.

Leeson, Peter T. and J. Robert Subrick (2006). "Robust Political Economy," *Review of Austrian Economics* 19: 107–111.

Lekniūtė, Zina, Roel Beetsma, and Eduard Ponds (2014). "U.S. Municipal Yields and Unfunded State Pension Liabilities," *Journal of Empirical Finance* 53: 15–32.

Lenze, David (2020). "Transactions of State and Local Government Defined Benefit Pension Plans: Experimental Estimates by States." *Bureau of Economic Analysis*. https://apps.bea.gov/scb/2020/07-july/0720-state-pension-estimates.htm.

Levy, David M. (2002). "Robust Institutions," *The Review of Austrian Economics* 15: 131–142.

Lu, Lina, Matthew Pritsker, Andrei Zlate, Kenechukwu Anadu, and James Bohn (2019). "Reach for Yield by US public pension funds," Financial and Economics Discussion Series, 2019–048, Washington: Board of Governors of the Federal Reserve System.

Lucas, Deborah J. and Stephen P. Zeldes (2009). "How Should Public Pension Plans Invest?" *The American Economic Review Papers and Proceedings* 99 (2): 527–532.

Malanga, Steven (2020). "Murphy's Bail-me-out Math" *City Journal*, June 3rd. www.city-journal.org/governor-murphy-threatening-huge-layoffs.

Mankiw, Gregory N. (2020). "The Puzzle of Low Interest Rates," New York Times, December 4th. www.nytimes.com/2020/12/04/business/low-interest-rates-puzzle.html.

Marks, Barry R., K. K. Raman, and Earl R. Wilson (1988). "Toward Understanding the Determinants of Pension Underfunding in the Public Sector," *Journal of Accounting and Public Policy* 7(3): 157–183.

Marlowe, Justin (2014). "Socially Responsible Investing and Public Pension Fund Performance," *Public Performance & Management Review*, 38(2): 337–358.

Martin, Adam and Diana Thomas (2013). "Two-Tiered Political Entrepreneurship and the Congressional Committee System," *Public Choice* 154: 21–37.

Matkin, David S. T., Gang Chen, and Hina Khalid (2019). "The Governance of Public Pensions: An Institutional Framework," *Administration & Society* 51 (1): 91–119.

Mennis, Greg, Susan Banta, and David Draine (2018). "Assessing the Risk of Fiscal Distress for Public Pensions: State Stress Test Analysis," M-RCBG Associate Working Paper Series No. 92. www.hks.harvard.edu/sites/default/files/centers/mrcbg/files/AWP_92_final.pdf

Miller, Randy and Rick Funston (2014). "Public Pension Governance That Works," Funston Advisory Services LLC. www.nasra.org/Files/Topical%20Reports/Governance%20and%20Legislation/FunstonGovernance1403.pdf.

Mitchell, Matthew and Nick Tuszynski (2012). "Institutions and State Spending: An Overview," *The Independent Review* 17(1): 35–49.

Mitchell, Olivia S. (1988). "Worker Knowledge of Pension Provisions," *Journal of Labor Economics* 6(1): 21–39.

Mitchell, Olivia S. and Ping-Lung Hsin. (1997). "Public Sector Pension and Governance and Performance." In Salavador Valdes Prieto (ed.), *The Economics of Pensions: Principles, Policies, and International Experience.* Cambridge: Cambridge University Press, pp.92–126.

Mitchell, Olivia S., David McCarthy, Stanley C. Wisniewski, and Paul Zorn (2001). "Developments in State and Local Pension Plans." In Olivia S. Mitchell and Edwin C. Hustead (eds.), *Pensions in the Public Sector.* University of Pennsylvania Press, pp.11–40.

Mitchell, Olivia S. and Robert S. Smith (1994). "Pension Funding in the Public Sector," *The Review of Economics and Statistics* 76(2): 278–290.

Modigliani, Franco and Merton H. Miller (1958). "The Cost of Capital, Corporation Investment And the Theory of Investment," *American Economic Review* 48: 261–297.

Moe, Terry (2011). *Special Interest: Teacher Unions and America's Public Schools.* Brookings Institute.

Monahan, Amy (2010). "Public Pension Plan Reform: The Legal Framework," *Education, Finance & Policy* 5. Minnesota Legal Studies Research No. 10–13.

Monahan, Amy B. (2012). "Statues as Contracts: The California Rule and Its Impact on Public Pension Reform," *Iowa Law Review* 97(4): 1029–1084.

Monahan, Amy B. (2015). "State Fiscal Constitutions and the Law and Politics of Public Pensions" *University of Illinois Law Review* 1: 117–174.

Morgenson, Gretchen (2017). "Strapped Pension Funds, and the Hefty Investment Fees They Pay," *New York Times*. May 12th. www.nytimes.com/2017/05/12/business/gretchen-morgenson-pension-funds-fees.html.

Moody's (2013). "Moody's Announces New Approach to Analyzing State, Local Government Pensions," *Moody's Investor Services*. www.moodys.com/research/Moodys-announces-new-approach-to-analyzing-statelocal-government-pensions–PR_271186.

Mourão, Paulo Reis (2007). "The Economics of Illusion: A Discussion Based on Fiscal Illusion," *Journal of Public Finance and Public Choice* 25(1): 67–86.

Munnell, Alicia H., Jean-Pierre Aubry, and Laura Quinby (2011). "Public Pension Funding in Practice," *Journal of Pension Economics and Finance* 10(2): 247–268.

Munnell, Alicia H. and Anqi Chen (2016). "New Developments in Social Investing by Public Pensions," *State and Local Pension Plans* 53 (November).

Munnell, Alicia H., Kelly Haverstick, Jean-Pierre Aubry, and Alex Gloub-Sass (2008). "Why Don't Some States and Localities Pay Their Required Pension Contributions?" *State and Local Pension Plans* 7 (May).

Munnell, Alicia H. and Annika Sundén (2001). "Investment Practices of State and Local Pension Funds." In Olivia S. Mitchell and Edwin C. Hustead (eds.), *Pensions in the Public Sector*. University of Pennsylvania Press, pp.153–174.

Muir, Dana M. (2016). "Decentralized Enforcement to Combat Financial Wrongdoing in Pensions: What Types of Watchdogs Are Necessary to Keep the Foxes Out of the Henhouse?" *American Business Law Journal* 53 (1): 33–96.

Naughton, James, Reining Petacchi and Joseph Weber (2015). "Public Pension Accounting Rules And Economic Outcomes," *Journal of Accounting and Economics* 59: 221–241.

National Association of State Retirement Administrators (2018). "Retirement Plan Options for State University Faculty and Staff." www.nasra.org/files/Compiled%20Resources/HigherEdPlanOptions.pdf.

National Association of State Retirement Administrators (2020). "Public Pension Plan Investment Return Assumptions," NASRA Issue Brief. www.nasra.org/files/Issue%20Briefs/NASRAInvReturnAssumptBrief.pdf.

National Conference of State Legislators (2017). "Full- and Part-Time Legislatures." June 14th. www.ncsl.org/research/aboutstatelegislatures/full-and-part-time-legislatures.aspx.

National Conference of State Legislators (2020). "Pension and Retirement Legislation Information by State." October 19th. www.ncsl.org/research/fiscal-policy/pension-legislation-database.aspx.

National Conference on Public Employee Retirement Systems (2020). "Auto-Triggers: Exploring Their Potential in the Public Pension Ecosystem. www .ncpers.org/files/NCPERS%202019%20Research%20Series_Auto-Triggers_Exploring%20Their%20Potential%20in%20the%20Public%20Pension%20Ecosystem_Web.pdf.

New Jersey Legislature, "Lottery Enterprise Contribution Act" P.L. 2017 c. 98. www.njleg.state.nj.us/2016/Bills/PL17/98_.PDF.

Nava, Victor (2014). "Did Pension Reform Fail in Alaska?" Reason Foundation, May 7th. https://reason.org/commentary/did-pension-reform-in-alaska-fail/.

Niskanen, William (1968). "The Peculiar Economics of Bureaucracy," *American Economic Review* 58(2): 293–305.

Norcross, Eileen (2010). "Fiscal Evasion in State Budgeting," Mercatus Working Paper 10(39), Mercatus Center at George Mason University.

Norcross, Eileen and Roman Hardgrave (2011). "Accounting for the Cost of a Public Sector Worker in New Jersey," Mercatus Working Paper 11 (38), Mercatus Center at George Mason University.

North, Douglass C. (1990). *Institutions, Institutional Change, and Economic Performance.* Cambridge University Press.

Novy-Marx, Robert (2013). "Logical Implications of GASB's Methodology for Valuing Pension Liabilities," *Financial Analysts Journal* 69(1): 26–32.

Novy-Marx, Robert, and Joshua D. Rauh (2009). "The Liabilities and Risks of State-Sponsored Pension Plans," *Journal of Economic Perspectives* 23(4): 191–210.

Novy-Marx, Robert and Joshua D. Rauh (2011). "Policy Options for State Pension Systems and Their Impact on Plan Liabilities," *Journal of Pension and Economic Finance* 10(2): 173–194.

Novy-Marx, Robert and Joshua Rauh (2014). "The Revenue Demands of Public Employee Pension Promises," *American Economic Journal: Economic Policy* 6(1): 193–229.

Oates, Wallace E. (1988). "On the Nature and Measurement of Fiscal Illusion: A Survey." In Geoffrey Brennan, Bhajan Singh Grewal, and Peter Groenewegen (eds.), *Taxation and Fiscal Federalism: Essays in Honour of Russel Mathews.* Sydney: Australian National University Press, pp.65–82.

Olson, Mancur (1965). *The Logic of Collective Action.* Harvard University Press.

Oosting, Jonathan (2017). "Synder signs Michigan teacher retirement reforms," *The Detroit News*, July 13th. www.detroitnews.com/story/news/politics/2017/07/13/school-pension-reform/103662102/.

Ostrom, Vincent (1997). *The Meaning of Democracy and the Vulnerabilities of Democracies*. University of Michigan Press.

Pauly, Mark V. (1968). "The Economics of Moral Hazard: Comment," *The American Economic Review* 58(3), Part I: 531–537.

Peng, Jun (2009). *State and Local Pension Fund Management*. Auerbach Publications.

Pennington, Mark (2011). *Robust Political Economy*. Cheltenham, UK and Northampton, MA: Edward Elgar Publishing.

Pension Protection Act of 2006 (2006). Public Law 109–280. www.govinfo.gov/content/pkg/PLAW-109publ280/pdf/PLAW-109publ280.pdf.

Pensions & Investments, "New Jersey OKs $4.7 billion payment to pension fund," by Robert Steyer, September 29, 2020. www.pionline.com/legislation/new-jersey-oks-47-billion-payment-pension-fund.

Picconi, Marc (2006). "The Perils of Pensions: Does Pension Accounting Lead Investors and Analysts Astray?" *The Accounting Review* 81(4): 925–955.

Politi, James and Colby Smith (2020). Fed Extends Municipal Lending to Smaller US Cities and Counties. *Financial Times*. April 27th. www.ft.com/content/34a77027-72b9-4a6b-9aa4-7cf9a6fa56e5.

Public Employees' Retirement System of New Jersey (2020). Actuarial Valuation Report as of July 1, 2019. www.nj.gov/treasury/pensions/documents/financial/actuarial2019/2019pers.pdf.

Puviani, Amilcare (1903). *Teoria della Illusione Finanziaria*. Remo Sandon.

Quinby, L. D., Aubry, J. P., and Munnell, A. H. (2020). Pensions for State and Local Government Workers Not Covered by Social Security: Do Benefits Meet Federal Standards? *Social Security Bulletin* 80(3): 1.

Rachel, Lukasz and Thomas D. Smith (2017). "Are Low Real Interest Rates Here to Stay?" *International Journal of Central Banking* 50(September): 1–42.

Randazzo, Anthony (2017). "There Is a Tangled Web of Factors Causing Inappropriate Pension Funding Behavior, *Journal of Law, Economics and Policy* 14(1): 107–126.

Rauh, Joshua (2017). "Hidden Debt, Hidden Deficits: 2017 Edition." www.hoover.org/research/hidden-debt-hidden-deficits-2017-edition.

Rauh, Joshua (2019). "Hidden Debt, Hidden Deficits: The 2019 Update," Stanford University's Hoover Institution. www.hoover.org/news/hidden-debt-hidden-deficits-2019-update.

Reitmeyer, John (2018). "Treasury Paid BOA $34 million to Shift Lottery to State Employee Pension Fund," *NJ Spotlight News*, January 11. www.njspotlight.com/2018/01/18-01-11-treasury-divulges-it-paid-boa-34m-to-shift-lottery-to-public-employee-pension-fund/.

Ricketts, Lowell R., and Christopher J. Walker (2012). "State and Local Debt: Growing Liabilities Jeopardize Fiscal Health," *The Regional Economist*.

Rose, Paul and Jason S. Seligman (2013). "Are Alternative Investments Prudent? Public Sector Pension Use and Fiduciary Duty," *Proceedings Annual Conference on Taxation and. Minutes of the Annual Meeting of the National Tax Association* 107: 1–34.

Roybark, Helen M., Edward N. Coffman, and Gary J. Previts (2012). "The First Quarter Century of the GASB (1984-2009): A Perspective on Standard Setting (Part One)," *ABACUS* 48(1): 1–30.

Russell, Nathan J. (2006). "An Introduction to the Overton Window of Political Possibilities," Mackinac Center. January 4th. www.mackinac.org/7504.

Schneider, Marguerite and Fariborz Damanpour (2001). "Determinants of Public Pension Plan Investment Return: The Role of Fund Value Maximization and Public Choice Theory," *Public Management Review* 3 (4): 551–573.

Scott, Neah (2019a). "The 2019 Regular Legislative Session Update," *The Advisor*, p. 1. July. www.rsa-al.gov/uploads/files/Advisor_July_19_web.pdf.

Scott, Neah (2019b). "Improving Benefits for RSA Tier II Employees," *The Advisor*, p. 1. August. www.rsaal.gov/uploads/files/Advisor_August_19_web.pdf.

Selby, Anna K (2011). "Pensions in a Pinch: Why Texas Should Reconsider its Policies on Public Retirement Benefit Protection," *Texas Tech Law Review* 43: 1211–1245.

Shen, Pu (2000). "The P/E Ratio and Stock Market Performance," *Economic Review*, Federal Reserve Bank of Kansas City 85 (Q IV): 23–36.

Shiller, Robert J. (2015). *Irrational Exuberance*. Revised and expanded 3rd ed. Princeton University Press.

Shughart, William F. II and Josh T. Smith (2020). "The Broken Bridge of Public Finance: Majority Rule, Earmarked Taxes and Social Engineering," *Public Choice* 183(3): 315–338.

Sidarova, Jen (2020). "Federal Bailout of Public Pension Systems Would Reward Some States After Decades of Mismanagement," Reason Foundation. April 30th. https://reason.org/commentary/federal-bailout-of-public-pension-systems-would-reward-some-states-after-decades-of-mismanagement/.

Skeel, David (2016). "Fixing Puerto Rico's Debt Mess," *The Wall Street Journal*. January 5th. www.wsj.com/articles/fixing-puerto-ricos-debt-mess-1452040144.

Smythe, Thomas I. Chris R. McNeil, and Philip C. English II (2015). "When Does CalPERS' Activism Add Value?" *Journal of Economics and Finance* 39: 641–660.

Sneed, Cynthia A. and John E. Sneed (1997). "Unfunded Pension Obligations as a Source of Fiscal Illusion for State Governments," *Journal of Public Budgeting, Accounting and Financial Management* 9(1): 5–20.

Society of Actuaries (2014). Report of the Blue Ribbon Panel on Public Pension Plan Funding. www.soa.org/globalassets/assets/files/newsroom/brp-report.pdf.

Somin, Ilya (2016). *Democracy and Political Ignorance*. Stanford University Press.

Somin, Ilya (2020). *Free to Move*. Oxford University Press.

Stalebrink, Odd J. (2014). "Public Pension Funds and Assumed Rates of Return: An Empirical Examination of Public Sector of Defined Benefit Pension Plans," *The American Review of Public Administration* 44(1): 92–111.

Stalebrink, Odd J. (2017). "Public Pension Fund Investments: The Role of Governance Structures," *Journal of Law, Economics and Policy* 14(1): 35–60.

Stalebrink, Odd J. and Peirre Donatella (2020). "Public Pension Governance and Opportunistic Accounting Choice: A Politico-Economic Approach," *The American Review of Public Administration*, forthcoming.

Starr-McCluer, Martha and Annika Sunden (1999). "Workers' Knowledge of Their Pension Coverage: A Reevaluation," Federal Reserve. www.federalreserve.gov/econresdata/scf/files/penknow.pdf.

The Pew Charitable Trusts and John Arnold Foundation (2014). "State Public Pension Investment Shift Over Past 30 Years." www.pewtrusts.org/~/media/assets/2014/06/state_public_pension_investments_shift_over_past_30_years.pdf.

The Pew Charitable Trusts (2015). "The State Pensions Funding Gap: Challenges Persist." www.pewtrusts.org/~/media/assets/2015/07/pewstates_statepensiondebtbrief_final.pdf.

The Pew Charitable Trusts (2019a). "Legal Protections for State Pension and Retiree Health Benefits: Findings from a 50-State Survey of Retirement Plans," *Issue Brief*, May. www.pewtrusts.org//media/assets/2019/05/prs_legal_protections_for_state_and_local_pension_and_retiree_medical_benefits_brief_final.pdf.

The Pew Charitable Trusts (2019b). "State Pension Funds Reduce Assumed Rates of Return," Issue Brief December 2019. www.pewtrusts.org/en/research-and-analysis/issue-briefs/2019/12/state-pension-funds-reduce-assumed-rates-of-return.

The Wall Street Journal (2007). "Pension Crash Landing." May 29th.

The Wall Street Journal (2020). "Hijacking the Fed to Bail Out States." December 17th.

Thom, Michael (2017). "The Drivers of Public Sector Pension Reform Across the U.S. States," *American Review of Public Administration*, 47(4): 431–442.

Thornburg, Steven W. and Kirsten M. Roasacker (2018). "Accounting, Politics, and Public Pensions," CPA Journal (May). www.cpajournal.com/2018/05/18/accounting-politics-and-public-pensions/.

Trevino, Ruben and Fiona Robertson (2002). "P/E Ratios and Stock Market Returns," *Journal of Financial Planning* 15(2): 76–84.

Triest, Robert K. and Bo Zhao (2014). "The Role of Economic, Fiscal, and Financial Shocks in the Evolution of Public Sector Pension Funding," *Proceedings of the Annual Conference on Taxation and Minutes of the Annual meeting of the National Tax Association* 107: 1–25.

Troesken, Werner (2006). *The Great Lead Water Pipe Disaster.* MIT Press.

Tullock, Gordon (1975). "The Transitional Gains Trap," *The Bell Journal of Economics* 6(2): 671–678.

Tullock, Gordon (2005). *Bureaucracy.* Liberty Fund Inc.

U.S. Senate (1984). "The Employee Retirement Income Security Act of 1974: The First Decade." www.aging.senate.gov/imo/media/doc/reports/rpt884.pdf.

Useem, Michael and Olivia S. Mitchell (2000). "Holders of the Purse Strings: Governance and Performance in Public Retirement Systems," *Social Science Quarterly* 81(2): 489–506.

Vermeer, Thomas E., Alan K. Styles, and Terry K. Patton (2010). "Are Local Governments Adopting Optimistic Actuarial Methods and Assumptions for Defined Benefit Pension Plans?" *Journal of Public Budgeting, Accounting & Financial Management* 22(4): 511–542.

Vock, Daniel C. and Liz Farmer (2016). "Alabama's One-Man Pension Show," *Governing.* May. www.governing.com/topics/mgmt/gov-alabama-david-bronner.html.

Wagner, Gary A. and Erick M. Elder (2021). "Campaigning for Retirement: State Teacher Union Campaign Contributions and Pension Generosity," *European Journal of Political Economy*, forthcoming.

Wagner, Richard E. (2007). *Fiscal Sociology and the Theory of Public Finance.* Edward Elgar.

Wagner, Richard E. (2015). "American Federalism." Mercatus Center at George Mason University. www.mercatus.org/system/files/Wagner-web.pdf.

Wang, Qiushi and Jun Peng (2016). "An Empirical Analysis of State and Local Public Pension Plan Funded Ratio Change, 2001-2009," *American Review of Public Administration* 46(1): 75–91.

Walsh, Mary Williams (2020). "Illinois Seeks a Bailout from Congress for Pension and Cities," *New York Times*, April 17th. www.nytimes.com/2020/04/17/business/dealbook/illinois-pension-coronavirus.html.

Waring, M. Barton (2012). *Pension Finance*. Wiley.

Wehrwein, Austin C. (1964). "Hoffa Convicted on the Use of Union Funds: Faces 20 Years," *New York Times*. July 27th. https://timesmachine.nytimes.com/timesmachine/1964/07/27/118671282.html?pageNumber=1.

Weinberg, Sheila and Eileen Norcross (2017). "A Judge in Their Own Cause: GASB 67/68 and the Continued Mismeasurement of Public Sector Pension Liabilities," *Journal of Law, Economics & Policy* 14(1): 61–94.

Weinberg, Sheila and Eileen Norcross (2017). "GASB 67 and GASB 68: What the New Accounting Standards Mean for Public Pension Reporting," *Mercatus on Policy* (June). www.mercatus.org/system/files/mercatus-weinberg-gasb-67-68-mop-2017-v1.pdf.

White, Lawrence (2005). "The Fed System's Influence on Research in Monetary Economics," *Econ Journal Watch* 2(2): 325–354.

Wittman, Donald (1995). *The Myth of Democratic Failure*. University of Chicago Press.

Wooten, James A. (2005). *The Employee Retirement Income Security Act of 1974: A Political History*. University of California Press.

Zorn, Paul (1997). "Public Pensions," *Public Administration Review* 57(4): 361–362.

About the Authors

Eileen Norcross is Vice President of Policy Research and Senior Research Fellow at the Mercatus Center at George Mason University. Her research focuses on questions of public finance, fiscal federalism, polycentric governance, and how institutions support or hamper economic resiliency and civil society. She is the lead author of *Ranking the States' Fiscal Condition*.

Her work has been cited in various media outlets, and her op-eds have appeared in the *Wall Street Journal*, the *New York Post, Christian Science Monitor, US News & World Report*, and *Forbes*.

Norcross has testified before Congress on the Community Development Block Grant program, state and local pension underfunding, municipal bankruptcy, and the use of technology to monitor stimulus funding. She has also testified on fiscal policies in Pennsylvania, Florida, California, New Hampshire, and Montana. She served as a public member on the Virginia Commission on Employee Retirement Security and Pension Reform from 2016 to 2017. Her academic publications include articles in the *Journal of Law, Economics, and Policy* (co-authored with Sheila Weinberg), the *Maryland Journal*, the *Review of Austrian Economics* (co-authored with Anne Hobson), and the *American Journal of Economics and Sociology* (co-authored with Paul Dragos Aligica), and a book chapter in *The Political Economy of Hurricane Katrina and Community Rebound*, edited by Emily Chamlee-Wright and Virgil Henry Storr.

Norcross received both her M.A. in economics and her B.A. in economics and American history from Rutgers University.

Daniel J. Smith is Director of the Political Economy Research Institute and Professor of Economics in the Jones College of Business at Middle Tennessee State University. He serves as the North American Co-editor of *The Review of Austrian Economics* and is President-elect of the Society for the Development of Austrian Economics.

His academic research and policy work uses Austrian and public choice economics to analyze private and public governance institutions. He is the co-author of *Money and the Rule of Law: Generality and Predictability in Monetary Institutions* (Cambridge University Press), written with Peter J. Boettke and Alexander W. Salter. His research is published in academics journals, such as *Public Choice, Economics of Governance*, and the *Quarterly Review of*

Economics and Finance, and in chapters in books published by Oxford University Press, Routledge, and Wiley-Blackwell.

Smith has published numerous op-eds in outlets across the nation, including in the *Wall Street Journal, The Hill, Investor's Business Daily*, and *CNBC.com*. Daniel received his M.A. and Ph.D. in economics from George Mason University and his B.B.A. in economics and finance from Northwood University.

Acknowledgments

Peter J. Boettke helped us develop and publish this Element; it won't have come to fruition without his support. Priya Samidurai and Karla Moran also played a vital role in publishing this Element. We also appreciate the comments from referees that helped us improve our manuscript.

We would also like to acknowledge our respective co-authors on our previously published public pension research: Rania Al-Bawwab, Andrew G. Biggs, Courtney A. Collins, John A. Dove, Olivia Gonzalez, Emily Hamilton, Roman Hardgrave, and Sheila Weinberg. That research was an important input into this Element. We also want to thank Rania Al-Bawwab for helpful research assistance.

In addition, Dan thanks the Political Economy Research Institute's Henrietta Bailey (Executive Aide) and Brian Delaney (Publication and Communications Editor) for assisting him with administrative work while writing this Element.

Cambridge Elements ≡

Austrian Economics

Peter Boettke
George Mason University
Peter Boettke is Professor of Economics & Philosophy at George Mason University, the BB&T Professor for the Study of Capitalism, and the director of the F. A. Hayek Program for Advanced Study in Philosophy, Politics and Economics at the Mercatus Center at George Mason University.

About the series
This series will primarily be focused on contemporary developments in the Austrian School of Economics and its relevance to the methodological and analytical debates at the frontier of social science and humanities research, and the continuing relevance of the Austrian School of Economics for the practical affairs of public policy throughout the world.

Cambridge Elements ☰

Austrian Economics

Elements in the series

The Political Economy of Public Pensions
Eileen Norcross and Daniel J. Smith

The Decline and Rise of Institutions
Liya Palagashvili, Ennio Piano and David Skarbek

Austrian Capital Theory: A Modern Survey of the Essentials
Peter Lewin and Nicolas Cachanosky

*Public Debt as a Form of Public Finance: Overcoming a Category Mistake and its
Vices*
Richard E. Wagner

The Origins and Consequences of Property Rights
Colin Harris, Meina Cai, Ilia Murtazashvili and Jennifer Brick Murtazashvili

A full series listing is available at: www.cambridge.org/core/series/elements-in-austrian-economics